Swing
Low

Swing Low

A Life

Miriam Toews

Arcade Publishing • New York

FIRST U.S. EDITION 2001

Originally published in Canada by Stoddart Publishing Co. Ltd.

Library of Congress Cataloging-in-Publication Data
  Toews, Miriam, 1964–
    Swing low : a life / Miriam Toews.
        p. cm.
    ISBN 1-55970-587-6
      1. Toews, Mel. 2. Manic-depressive persons—Biography.
    3. Mennonites—Biography. 4. Teachers—Biography. I. Title.
    RC516 .T64 2001
    616.89'5'0092—dc21
    [B]   2001022672

Published in the United States by Arcade Publishing, Inc., New York
Distributed by Time Warner Trade Publishing

Visit our Web site at www.arcadepub.com

10 9 8 7 6 5 4 3 2 1

PRINTED IN THE UNITED STATES OF AMERICA

For Mel

In the end, one can give only one look upwards,
give one breath outwards. At that moment a man probably
surveys his whole life. For the first time — and the last time.

— Franz Kafka

Acknowledgements

A *special note of thanks to my sister, Marj Toews*, who has guided me through the writing of this book with such careful precision, patience, wisdom, and love. And to my mom, Elvira, whose courage, compassion, and enormous capacity for joy inspire me daily. And to my husband, Cassady, for his endless generosity of spirit in good times and in bad. Thanks also to my editor, Don Bastian, for his expert advice and encouragement all along the way. Thank you.

And, for their support, my sincere gratitude to the Manitoba Arts Council and the Canada Council for the Arts.

Prologue

"Nothing accomplished."

I don't know what my father meant when he said it. I had asked him, the day before he took his own life, what he was thinking about, and that was his reply. Two hopeless words, spoken in a whisper by a man who felt he had failed on every level. This book is my attempt to prove my father wrong.

At the age of seventeen, he was diagnosed as suffering from the mental illness known then as manic depression and today as bipolar disorder. His method of self-defence, along with the large amounts of medication he was prescribed, was silence. And maybe, for him, it worked. He managed, against the advice of his psychiatrist, to get married, to rear a family, and to teach elementary school for more than forty years. His psychiatrist warned him, way back in the early 1950s, that the odds of living a normal life were heavily stacked against him. In fact, Dad's life fell into the typical pattern of our small town of Steinbach, Manitoba: an ordered existence of work, church, and family, with the occasional inevitable upsets along the way. His managing to live an ordinary life was an extraordinary accomplishment. It is a measure of his strength, his high (some would say impossibly high) personal standards, and his extreme self-discipline that he managed to stay sane, organized, and ordinary for so long.

A year or so after his retirement, my parents went out for a drive in the countryside around town. "Well," said my father after they'd driven in silence for a while, "I did it." "You've done many things, Mel," said my mom. "What are you referring to?" "I did what they said I would never do," answered my father.

And he did it exceptionally well. He became a much-loved and respected teacher, known especially for his kindness, exuberance, and booming voice, and at home my mother and my sister and I had everything we could possibly want or need. There was only one thing we missed, and that was hearing him speak. I have often wondered what he would have said about himself, if he had spoken. He never talked about his past, even his childhood, and often he simply didn't speak at all. His whole world, it seemed, was in the classroom. And when there, he gave it his all. My sister and I, both students of his at one time, used to sit in class in absolute awe. Was this funny, energetic, outspoken man really our father? It must have been teaching, the daily ritual of stepping outside himself and into a vital role, that sustained him all those years.

Had we known then what we know now, we would have understood that the end of his teaching career would, essentially, mean the end of Mel. After his suicide, we were left with many questions. How could this have happened? we asked ourselves over and over. After all, other people have difficulty retiring, but they don't necessarily kill themselves. I became obsessed with knowing all that I could about his life, searching, I suppose, for clues that would ultimately lead me to the cause of his death. With the help of my mother and my sister and Dad's friends, colleagues, and relatives, I've managed to put a few pieces of the puzzle of his life together. But in spite of many theories and much speculation, there's really only one answer, and that is depression. A clinical, profoundly inadequate word for deep despair.

At the end of his life, my father, in a rare conversation, asked me to write things down for him, words and sentences that would lead him out of his confusion and sadness to a place and time that he might understand. "You will be well again," I wrote. "Please write that again," he'd ask. I wrote many things over and over and over, and he would read each sentence, each declaration and piece of information out loud. Eventually, it stopped making sense to him. "You will be well again?" he'd ask me, and I'd say, "No, Dad, *you* will be well again." "I will be well again?" he'd ask. "Yes," I'd say. "I will be well again," he'd repeat. "Please write that down."

Soon I was filling up pages of yellow legal notepads with writing from his own point of view so he could understand it when he read it to himself. After his death, when I began writing this book, I continued to write in the same way. It was a natural extension of the writing I'd done for him in the hospital, and a way, though not a perfect one, of hearing what my father might have talked about if he'd ever allowed himself to. If he'd ever thought it would matter to anybody.

After his death, I read everything I could find on mental illness and suicide, poring over facts and statistics, survivors' accounts, reasons, clues, anything at all that might help me to understand, or if not to understand then at least to accept, my father's decision and to live with it. By dragging some of the awful details into the light of day, they became much less frightening. I have to admit, my father didn't feel the same way, but he found a way to alleviate his pain, and so have I.

Swing
Low

*B*ethesda Hospital, Steinbach, Manitoba. I've been trying for weeks to make sense of things. For instance, why am I here? I've filled up several yellow legal pads, right to the margins, with words and sentences and sentence fragments, but nothing is clear to me. It seems, upon rereading my notes, that I've written several things repeatedly, such as "Develop a new life strategy." That particular sentence appears on almost every page, as do hearts (I'm drawing hearts!) with the words "I love" inside them. I suppose I've forgotten the names of those I love or I haven't drawn the hearts big enough to hold them all or I'm simply confirming with myself my ability to love. It bothers me that I haven't put the names in.

Two days ago I decided to test my younger brother, who runs this hospital. He sat at the foot of my bed watching me and I sat at the head of my bed watching him. (What was there to say?) Eventually I blurted out, I'm mentally ill. I said it because I wanted him to say that I wasn't or that, if I was, I would soon be fine, that life was like this for a lot of people from time to time, that I wasn't alone, that I had nothing to be ashamed of, and that I'd be just as right as rain in no time.

My brother answered, Yes, you are. No more and no less, a brief (life) sentence hanging in the air between us like a raised fist. I sat on my bed and stared out the window. Eventually my brother went on a bit to say that he felt my "admission" was a big step forward, an essential part of the healing process, and now, perhaps, I'd be able to open up with my psychiatrist. You've got to be honest, Mel, he said. And of course he's right. But one must find the words first, and words don't come as easily to me.

And I don't mean to sound disrespectful, but the thing is there is no psychiatrist here for me to "open up with." I would like to ask my brother when and if I'll see one, but I can't find the right words to do that either and I'm ashamed besides. Rather, we spend our time staring at one another. And the days go by. Reg told me that he has a difficult choice to make, that is whether to treat me as a brother would or as a regional health authority CEO would, and he has chosen "brother," which means he comes to visit but doesn't interfere with my hospital care. I guess that makes sense, it sounds nice, but I would have preferred it had he chosen "CEO," because after all I do have a family, and what I need, at least according to Reg, is a shrink to be honest with, and I could use a plug from him, an endorsement rather, and so . . . perhaps he could produce one for me, because I think I would like to get some help. I mean, it's wonderful that he's being brotherly, but it raises the question then of who's in charge of me here. In the meantime,

I've decided to write a few things down. Things about myself, my life, etc., so that when my time comes to open up, if it should, I'll have a bit of an idea of what to say.

Bethesda Hospital, Steinbach, Manitoba, Date: find newspaper, determine date, insert here. (The custodian brings the newspaper to me every morning. He is a friend of mine and former custodian of Elmdale School.)

∽

I'm a methodical man so this business re losing my mind is frustrating. I keep records of everything, every transaction, every purchase, every drawing my children ever made, every notebook they filled as students. Everything. But they're not doing me much good now.

In my travel diaries I record seating orders: wife, Elvira, and daughter Miriam, left side of six-seater plane. Pilot, myself, and other daughter, Marj, on right side. Wind coming from the north, Elvira decked out in colourful new pantsuit, gas gauge at halfway mark, etc. I wrote my own textbook on Canadian history when I found the existing province-issued text to be inadequate. I have three filing cabinets with file folders precisely labelled and carefully maintained. In my safety deposit box I have kept, for forty-two years, the receipt for the wedding rings my wife and I bought at Birks Jewellers, and also the receipt from the hotel we stayed in on our wedding night . . . eleven dollars. I didn't sleep at all that night. Not for a second. I was a wreck. I willed my hands to stop trembling. I would have shouted at them if I hadn't been worried about waking Elvira. I'm rather a nervous man, prone to panic attacks and nail-biting. I worry.

There are two things that help to dispel my nervous energy: writing and walking. Once, years ago, I stopped walking and lay down in my bed for several months. Once, very recently, I went for a walk and ended up in a town twenty miles away. When I say writing I mean writing down facts and details and lists and instructions to myself. I've been researching the lives of important Canadians such as Emily Carr, Lucy Maud Montgomery, and Foster Hewitt. By writing down the details of the lives of these accomplished individuals, I learn how to live.

I should add that part of the reason, beyond my own obvious limitations, for the interrupted feel of my writing has to do with the nurses who come into my room from time to time with questions and drinks and pills and clipboards. They have become curious about my writing, and every time they come into my room I stop and nod and smile pleasantly. Occasionally I'll say something like Keep up the good work, or, Quite an efficient system you've got here, which isn't necessarily true, but I like to offer encouragement when I can.

When I begin to write again I have often forgotten entirely what I was writing about. Several of the nurses are former students of mine and still call me Mr. Toews. The nurse who attached the wander guard to my wrist reminded me of the year we built a replica Hudson Bay Trading Post and operated it as a real store for the entire school year. I still have the photographs, she said, and offered to bring them in to show me. I told her I'd like that. Some of the nurses are mothers of former students of mine and will tell me what their children are doing these days. When I was first admitted to the hospital last night or two weeks or eight years ago, I spoke to the nurses at length. I asked them questions such as Where am I? Why am I here? Where is my wife? (this last over and over and over) until they grew short with me. I noticed that one nurse had written on her clipboard, "Patient talks non-stop, obviously wants attention." Many of them, however, know their boss is my brother, and they try hard not to get angry with me. I'm grateful for every kindness.

But this business of "wanting attention" embarrassed me to such an extent that I vowed to remain quiet. Besides, it wasn't attention I wanted so much as clarification. But they're busy, these nurses, and I understand that I baffle them. I baffle myself. As for walking, my second-favourite chaos-dispelling activity, they frown on it. They're afraid I won't come back. (And yet they don't know why I'm here.) After I was admitted for the second time, they attached a wander guard to my wrist, a little device that makes a bell ring at the nursing station should I get as far as the front door. I had actually escaped previously; that's why they put the wander guard on me. The nurses promised my older daughter, Marj, that I would not be discharged over the weekend. He will tell you he's fine, she said, and he will be convincing, but please don't believe him. There's nobody at the house, my mother is exhausted and on the verge of having a nervous breakdown herself (from taking care of me they don't say) and is staying in the city for the weekend. Please don't let him go home.

They promised they wouldn't. In less than an hour I was out of there.

It didn't turn out well. I don't know exactly what happened or why I have these painful blisters on my feet. Naturally I asked but a well-meaning nurse in training mistook me for a large four-year-old and said, Oh, you've been a busy guy in the last couple of days. Busy, adds a doctor, having a psychotic breakdown. All I knew is that everything blew apart in my brain.

It's extremely difficult to get a straight answer around here. I imagine I walked for several miles before returning to my empty house, or that I returned first and then went for a fifteen-mile walk around and around town, I don't know. I can't find Elvira. In any case, I'm back in my brother's care for a while, and my daughters are very upset that I was allowed to leave in the first place. I suppose they didn't want me to see the blood or to find out the truth about Elvira. I am still not being told where my wife is, other than "in the city, resting," and I suspect she is dead. I suspect I have killed her. A friend came to see me and told me that on the day I was accidentally discharged he had given me a ride for several blocks, and we chatted like old times, but I don't remember that. My brother told my younger daughter, Miriam, that I smell bad. Thankfully I shifted into my catatonic gaze at nothing to save him the embarrassment of thinking I'd heard. Also, I'm not sure why there is blood on my kitchen floor, or whose it is. I asked him where Elvira is and he said the girls had told him she was very, very tired. And in the city, resting.

I don't believe him. I don't believe anybody. What I do believe is that I have accomplished nothing in my life, nothing at all. I have neglected my children and I have killed my wife. There is nothing left to do now but record the facts, as I always have.

I was born, in this very hospital, maybe even in this very room, on May 31, 1935, in the middle of the Great Depression (how apt) in the same year that Elvis Presley was born in Tupelo, Mississippi. I include that fact for no other reason than because I read it in the hospital copy of the *Winnipeg Free Press* just this very morning. That's part of my regular morning routine. That and checking on my friend Hercules in the hallway, and making a few rounds of my own. Checking up on morale.

And then what? I suppose I just lived, as a baby, with my parents and my older sister, here in Steinbach. A little to the north and west of Steinbach is the city of Winnipeg, to the south the border to the United States, to the east the lakes and rocky terrain of the Whiteshell Provincial Park and also a forest called the Sandilands. Directly west is farmland, very fertile, the best in the country, sunflowers, canola, alfalfa, you name it. In the middle of all of this sits Steinbach, a wealthy, industrious town of ten thousand or so, settled by several Mennonite families in the late 1800s. The Mennonite communities on this, the east side of the Red River, are called Ditzied, in Low German meaning "this side." The Mennonite communities on the other side of the Red are called Yantzied, meaning "that side." Of course, to the Mennonites living on the west side of the river, it is just the opposite. Both sides believe that those from Yantzied are less sophisticated and more religiously conservative. Naturally it's an argument with no end.

My grandfather, a baby at the time, was the youngest member of the "migration" that made its way from Russia to this patch of land promised to them by Queen Victoria and given to them for nothing by a government eager to have the land farmed and settled. He came close to dying and was nearly pitched overboard on the way. The Mennonites have a long history of moving from place to place in search of religious freedom. Here, apparently, they have found it. Thousands of Mennonites who stayed behind, in Russia, were eventually killed by the army, but some managed to escape. My friend Henry, for instance, fled Russia as a child sometime during World War Two and spent years wandering through Europe with his mother. The last thing I remember knowing about Henry — he told me this himself, at a barbecue — was that he had leased a brand-new Ford Saturn with an excellent mileage and maintenance policy.

When I was two I choked on a peanut and my mother said that incident might have shifted the fault lines in my brain and made me the anxious man that I am today.

When I was three and a half years old I was sent to the neighbours' with a message. My baby sister had died, and thank you very much for the soup. Did you thank her for the soup? my mother asked me when I got home. Yes. You were polite, then? Yes. And the other message? Yes. A year later my little brother was born to take my dead sister's place, and my mother, understandably, doted on him. She made it very clear to me and my older sister, Diana, that we were never to feed him peanuts or ice cubes. Nobody had ever told me that I'd had an incident with an ice cube, and in fact I think my mother made it up on the spot, but I appreciated her including it in the short list of banned treats for the baby. In my four-year-old way of thinking, addled, mind you, by the peanut incident, I saw my mother's inclusion of the words "and ice cubes" as a tender gesture meant to relieve some of the burden I felt as a person my little brother should not come to resemble. Don't choke on a peanut, you'll turn out like Mel. Oh, and also avoid . . . ice cubes! In my mind there were hundreds of little boys like myself who had had incidents with ice cubes and were just as guilty of being "off" as I was, and so I felt less responsible and less alone, and I was grateful to my mother for reducing some of the pressure I felt at the time.

～

Speaking of babies, there's one outside my room, directly across from the nursing station. Only in a rural hospital would a psychiatric patient and a premature baby be housed next to one another. They need to watch him very closely. His name is Hercules and he weighs a little less than four pounds, although the nurses tell me he's gaining weight nicely. My concern for Hercules has made me so nervous that I often stand next to his crib and stare at him for lengthy periods, while I wait for a meal or a visitor or for 9:30, when I make my regular call to the city. Should he be sleeping for this long? I'll ask the nurses. Yes, Mr. Toews, he's fine. Should this tube be under his mattress like this? Yes, Mr. Toews, relax. Excuse me, but, uh, Hercules looks uncomfortable. Okay, Mr. Toews, we'll be right there. Very good, I'll say, very good. If I'm in my room writing, as I am now, and I hear one of his machines beeping, I'll jump up and rush over to his crib. We're on it, Mel, the nurses will say, or, Mel, you're a little jumpy today.

Yes, well . . . there isn't much to do here. Yesterday I asked one daughter how long I'd been here. About ten days, she answered. Ten days! I said. That's rather long! There was so much to be done back at the house, I said, the flowers, the yard, the packing. I know, she said, everything's being taken care of, all you have to do is rest. Don't worry about a thing, okay? Everything's going to be okay. I promise. I promise. Then I'd launch into the Where is Mom? Where is Mom? Is she dead? And daughters tell me she isn't, only resting, only very, very tired. I have vowed to get better. It's my fault she's tired, but daughters tell me it's not, nobody's to blame. Tell her I love her, I say, and they promise they will. She loves you too, Dad, we all do. Sometimes I think I have spoken to her on the telephone. The girls say, You have! You have! Every morning at 9:30 you talk to her on the phone. She tells you she loves you and you tell her you love her. You ask if she's getting some rest. Yesterday you talked about baseball. You talk to her! Don't you remember?

Well, sometimes. I've written it down so that I will remember. Elvira loves me. So do the girls. I love. I love. In hearts, like a schoolboy. The girls say we'll get through this. The girls say the yard is fine and the income tax is done. The girls say nobody in town blames me. The girls say the car insurance is paid. They say the air conditioner has been fixed. They say we will be together again soon, very soon. That's another thing I write down a lot. They say we will be together again soon. Sometimes the girls write it down for me, when I can't, in big block letters on my yellow legal pads. WE LOVE YOU. MOM LOVES YOU. THIS IS NOT YOUR FAULT. YOU ARE A GOOD FATHER. WE ARE PROUD OF YOU. PLEASE TRY TO REST. PLEASE DON'T WORRY. YOU'LL BE TOGETHER WITH MOM SOON. PLEASE BELIEVE US. WE LOVE YOU AND ALWAYS WILL.

Yesterday my daughter shouted in the hallway outside my

room: When will he be seen by a psychiatrist? Shouldn't he be transferred to a psychiatric hospital? He's told you he wants to be helped! When will he get it?

I am absolutely mortified to hear this and I am worried that Hercules will be woken up by the shouting and that my brother will hear it too and be embarrassed. When I hear my daughters discussing my situation I try not to listen. Often, to distract myself from the goings-on in the hallway outside my room, I focus on the objects in my room.

I have several of what the nurses call my personal effects with me. A painting, by my granddaughter, of a red sailboat, yellow sails, blue sky, entitled "Summer Memories." There is one tiny figure on the deck of the boat. I've stuck it on my dresser mirror, under the tiny clasps that keep the glass secured. I also have a book of poetry given to me by Elvira before I was hospitalized. The poet was one of my first students, a man now more than fifty years old with grown children of his own. I have a lovely handmade glass vase with several yellow tulips in it, on the windowsill, and two very large Snickers bars on my bedside table.

I also have tracts, given to me by various visitors, and a Bible and a devotional book on Corinthians and a brochure advertising a new housing development on the edge of town. On one of my walks, after the wander guard was removed, I stopped in at the model home they use as an office and picked one up, for no reason whatsoever. I show it to my visitors from time to time, hoping to divert the conversation away from me, and often my visitors will indulge me and we'll chat, awkwardly, about the pros and cons of another housing development such as the one described in the brochure.

⤸

I took what they call a kitchen test the other day. I'm not sure why. The results? Patient is able to make toast but is unable to remember how to operate a can opener. A secret: I've never known how to operate a can opener. You gasp, it's shocking, I know. I lied to the kitchen testers. I took advantage of my forgetfulness and told them that operating a can opener was simply another thing I'd forgotten how to do. Oh, the subversive pleasure I, as an elementary school teacher, got from lying on my kitchen test . . . I have told a few other white lies during my stay in the hospital, it seemed simpler. How are you, Mel? Fine, fine. Be sure to say hello to Jake for me. Is he still enjoying his work at the printers? Oh, for sure, Mel, he misses you coming in with the *Class News*. Wonders when your next project will be ready. Oh, I'm working on it, Mrs. H., I am, I just need a little time.

I can't remember what Jake looks like. I suspect Mrs. H. is irritated with me, I miss Elvira. I don't want to open cans of tomato soup. I don't want to borrow ten dollars from my daughter, I don't want an old man's haircut at the personal care home, and I don't want to have to ask for clean underwear. My driver's licence has been taken from me, my belongings are packed away in boxes. I don't have another project, Mrs. H.

My students and I published newspapers every year. Roving reporters investigating the birth of a litter of kittens at the Penner farm, Jason's second broken arm in less than eight weeks, a trip to B.C., a family wedding, the death of a beloved pet, all the comings and goings of my group of eleven- and twelve-year-olds. The *Class News*. Stacks of paper arranged around the ping-pong table, I'd collate them all night long, around and around the ping-pong table, my tie tucked in between the buttons of my shirt, my sleeves rolled up, my family asleep upstairs, oblivious, thousands of copies to be delivered through town the next morning, eagerly anticipating the expression on my students' faces when they would see their words, their lives, in print! It was marvellous! To create a permanent written document bearing witness to real life, better than a thousand photographs, it was out of this world.

My senses were activated by the words describing the events rather than by the events themselves. I put a lot of stock in words, in written words.

Have just received my medication in a tiny paper cup. The nurse stands beside me until I take it. I swallow, smile, hand her the cup, and she says, Good.

Nothing I see is familiar and the parts of my body are strange, as though they belong to somebody else. My brain is stuck and every last ounce of energy I have is trying to get it out of its rut like a car stuck in snow. Forward, reverse, forward, reverse. How to explain the process of putting the pieces of my brain together: as though I'm attempting to walk down a street and various limbs, arms and legs, continue to drop off my body. I'm getting nowhere. Certain memories run through my mind on an endless tape loop, over and over and over. When I was a boy I had my tonsils removed. I was put under with chloroform and I dreamt I was somersaulting through the walls of the hospital. I still recall the feeling. It remains the most vivid dream of my entire life. Over and over and over, like this, and through. What a feeling.

When I was a boy I spent a great deal of time sitting in a homemade airplane in a blue shed behind the J.R. Friesen garage. On one of the airplane's wings were painted the letters CFAMV. I played with the control panel, and when it crashed in a neighbour's field I wasn't in it, but I was sure my fiddling with the buttons had made it crash and kill the man who was, I asked God to forgive me for killing the pilot and to wash away my sins with Jesus' blood.

When I was a boy I worked for my dad, taking care of chickens and sometimes having to kill them. I tried to convince myself that they deserved to die, that they were bad chickens, sinners, and that I was doing the right thing. I was once so unbelievably young.

⟨✿⟩

I nodded to a tall older man in my room just now and he nodded back. Then I noticed that I was staring at my reflection in the mirror, just beneath "Summer Memories." Excruciating! Is there a doctor in the house?! (Answer: Yes, but you baffle him. He prefers problems he can see. Am beginning to understand why.)

✿

Daughter says to doctor in hallway outside room: This is the second time my father has been in this hospital without receiving any type of care whatsoever. Where is the psychiatrist?

Answer: He retired this afternoon.

Daughter: This is a farce! Why won't you transfer him to the city? To a hospital with a psychiatric ward?

Answer: We think he might be ready to go home.

Daughter: *Home!* There's nobody *at* home! How can you let him go home after what happened?

Answer: Where is your mother? (Excellent question. I listen very closely after this.)

Daughter: In the city! She's exhausted, she can't take care of him anymore without help or she'll die, literally! He won't eat! He won't talk! He won't wash!

Answer: He talks here, some. He eats. He washes. He gets dressed. He's very cooperative, actually, very pleasant. Your father's an intelligent man. Perhaps you underestimate him.

Daughter: Because he wants to go home, that's why he's —

Answer: Then perhaps he should.

Daughters cry. Doctor must carry on with his rounds. Will stop in on his way back. Why? shouts daughter. For what? One daughter shushes other daughter. They will soon come into my room with their lies and their smiles and their hugs and kisses. We'll write things down together in big block letters (I haven't the heart to tell them I'm not blind) and I hope they don't leave too soon. One of my daughters has been wearing the same outfit now for several days, in fact it's been almost two weeks. Cut-off jeans, a blue tank top with a greenish flowered blouse over it. This morning I asked her if she had much trouble deciding what to wear and she said, Why? You don't like it? She didn't get my joke, and I answered, Oh no, I like it very much.

❦

I've heard a noise. There's a child in the hallway, apparently. It sounds as though a ball is being thrown against my door. Thump, thump, ka-thump. Now it's stopped. Now it's started again. Stopped. Started. The child is young and the ball gets away from him. He retrieves it and begins to throw it against my door again. He loses it, it rolls a little down the hall, he runs after it and brings it back . . . thump, thump. How will I write with all this racket going on?

Now I've lost the image of the child outside my door, but I can still hear the ball bouncing. The image has been replaced with another, it's a boy shooting baskets in the driveway! I know him!

I've just had visitors, my sister, Diana, and her husband. When they came in, authoritatively and all smiles, I said: Where's your basketball? (This sort of thing does NOT help my case.)

A woman has come into my room with more tracts and has asked me if I would be interested in crafts.

What sort of crafts? I asked. I failed the kitchen test, you know.

Kitchen table crafts, she said. We have lots of fun with oh, Popsicle sticks, doilies, pipe cleaners . . .

Before she could finish I applied catatonic gaze, willing her to leave, which she did but only after telling me crafts would do me good.

❧

Where were we? Well, let me begin again as a boy. I delivered the messages to the neighbours when I was three years old.

❧

My brain is still stuck. I meant to write about myself as a boy but . . . reverse, forward, reverse, forward, reverse . . . flooded. So, I've been looking out my window for hours at my late brother-in-law's home. In one spectacularly lucid moment a day or eight ago I remembered every detail of the obituary I had written for him while he lay dying years ago in this very hospital. I would rush to his bedside after work and pull up a chair while he added to and amended the details from our discussion of his obituary the day before. He always wanted it to be longer. He told me there were three things he'd like to do before he left this world: drive his company's cement truck one more time, have one more game of tennis, and make love to his wife.

You know, I told the nurse after my shower, when I was a child I dreamt I somersaulted through the hospital walls.

Did you really? she asked me.

I really dreamt it, yes, I answered. To this day it remains a vivid memory, as though it happened just yesterday.

There we go, Mr. T., we don't want you getting lost.

The funny thing is, I said, I feel that I already am.

Oh, that is funny, she agreed. Try to have a little rest.

My desk is littered with notes to myself, my file reads. I saw my file when the nurse put her clipboard down on my bedside table while she removed the dressings from my feet. I object to the use of that word "littered." Were they implying that these notes were worthless? That they belonged in the waste paper basket?

Why, then, when they don't want to listen to me, do they allude to my writing as garbage? When I speak I irritate and when I write I litter? How would they prefer I express myself, I wonder. With Popsicle sticks? I could have talked to myself, I suppose, but why raise another thousand eyebrows? It is interesting that I have used the word "myself" three times in the last two paragraphs and have no idea what it means anymore. (What does one do with pipe cleaners?)

By now it is quite dark outside. A light rain is falling. I smell lilacs. Or I smell something that reminds me of lilacs and of my hometown in May (this is my hometown in May) and especially the walk down First Street and then up William and finally across Main to the school. Every spring my desk was swamped with lilacs. Children brought me jam jars and ice cream pails and plastic honey tubs, whatever empty containers they could get their hands on, filled with lilacs, until I began running out of space for them and I'd have to beg the children to stop.

I like to imagine that the teacher has left the room inside my brain and every last neuron is out of its seat and acting up. I will walk in and ask them to take their seats, and miraculously they will.

Does it matter? Not everything does matter so much after all. When I was a young man I vacillated wildly between thinking everything mattered, that every word, every action, every task was important, to thinking that nothing at all mattered, that everything was futile. I had a gambler's mentality, all or nothing. Just as I appeared close to achieving normalcy and balance to a point where I could say Life is Good, I would notice myself cracking under the pressure of its goodness. Is this the sort of thing my doctor wants to hear? Should I ring my bell and have the nurse run in here so I can tell her that sometimes I think things matter and sometimes I think they don't? What does a ham have to do around here to get cured?

Keep writing. I had intended to review my life as a movie but I can see now that it's not fitting nicely into that format. It has all the structure of a bamboo hut in a hurricane and I must apologize for this lack of cohesion. A series of jerky stills, courtesy my renegade mind, will have to do. Just wait for the inevitable upside-down slide in the carousel. Why don't you run downstairs and make yourselves some popcorn while

I repair the reel. Oh, but there we go, I imagine you running and the image creates a tiny spark. I remember now.

When I was a boy I loved to run. One day I was out running all over town, through people's yards and up and down back lanes and empty streets, when I happened to come across an apple pie cooling on the wide wooden railing of Mr. and Mrs. I.Q. Unger's back porch. I was about nine and I should have known better, but I decided to take the pie and run. I had visions of myself enjoying a huge feast for one somewhere in the bush outside of town. I turned around to make sure I hadn't been followed and there, peering out from behind an old shed in the yard, was my little brother, the one I mentioned earlier, the one who replaced my dead sister, the one who stole my mother's heart.

What are you doing? he asked me, in Low German.

Nothing, I said, go away.

You're supposed to come home now, he said, you're supposed to stop all this running and come home.

I looked back at my pie. It was a perfect pie, light beige strips of dough criss-crossed on the top, bubbles of baked apple oozing through the tiny squares, columns of steam rising up from it.

Get lost, I said quietly, again in Low German.

My brother stepped out from behind the shed and slowly took aim at me with a homemade slingshot. I laughed.

Come with me right now or I'll shoot this thing, he said in a menacing voice.

Ha ha, I said, hoping the people inside the house wouldn't hear us.

My brother took a few steps towards me and said, I mean it, I'll shoot you. I could see the ugly little rock he had placed up against the elastic, holding it between his finger and thumb. He was only four or five years old.

I smiled at him and made a face. He came closer. I didn't

move. Finally he was only a few steps away from me and still he kept coming closer, pointing that homemade slingshot at my face and telling me to come home. Right now, he said, over and over again in a whisper. Right now.

I stepped backwards. He came closer. I took another step backwards, towards my pie, and another step, hoping, in one fluid motion, to grab the pie, leap over the porch railing, and avoid getting shot by my brother.

At this point he was so close to me I could have reached out and grabbed the slingshot, but my brother had it cocked and ready to fire. All he had to do was let go. I took one more step backwards, thinking that it would buy me another second or two to formulate my plan, but that's when the plan died.

The heel of my shoe caught between the slats of the railing, and in an effort to pull it free I lost my balance and fell on my stomach. The pie, perched precariously on the rickety railing, fell too, right onto my back, face up, intact and still perfect. But irretrievable. As my brother stood beside me laughing, I frantically tried to grab at the pie burning a hole into my back.

My shoe was still caught, preventing me from rolling over, and anyway, if I had rolled over the pie would have slid off my back and been ruined and at that point I was still hoping to eat it.

Richard, I hissed, get the pie off me! I'll share it with you, I promise. Please!

I was in agony. I imagined the skin melting off my back and the pie dropping into a cavity next to ribs and kidneys and whatever else was in there. My brother, however, was thoroughly entertained and had no intention of ending the show by helping me out.

Please, I begged him. I could have wriggled on my stomach and the pie would have fallen off but still I harboured a faint hope that the pie would be mine and I didn't want to pick pieces of it off the dusty wooden floor of that old porch.

Just then Mrs. Unger, the pie-baker and owner of the property on which I lay twitching and smouldering and begging for mercy, opened her back door and stepped onto the porch.

Richard shrieked and fled and Mrs. Unger ran back inside for oven gloves. Seconds later she had removed the pie, then hammered my foot out from between the slats, sat me down at her kitchen table, and was preparing a soothing ointment of aloe vera and something else to pack on my smoked hide.

I cried, shamelessly, and her old husband held out his stiff handkerchief. After treating my back, Mrs. Unger gave me a large piece of that apple pie with ice cream and after that she gave me another, smaller piece. I ate very slowly and she asked me, in Low German, if I needed to stay away from home for a while.

I told her no, no, that in fact I must return immediately, that I had a lot of work to do, and my parents would be wondering where I was. Mrs. Unger told me that she had often seen me running, was I training for the Olympics? she asked. Then she added that if I ever needed a destination, her door was always open. Her husband piped up and said he would put a sign up over the door that said Finish Line. The three of us chuckled and in all the years to follow, never once spoke of my attempted pie theft.

⟡

The word "home" induces such nostalgia these days it makes my head hurt. I imagine that I am massive and hovering somewhere in the sky with a bird's-eye view of Canada. Gradually my vision narrows and all I can see is the province of Manitoba, all the way from Hudson Bay through the Inter-lake, down to the prairie farms and towns of the south. But then my vision narrows again and all I can see is the town of Steinbach, my town, with its many churches and cars and split-level stucco homes, and then the vise grip again and all that appears is my home, what used to be my home, and then even that disappears and all I can see is my kitchen table, where my daughters and my wife are seated and having an animated conversation, and then zoom, the only thing I see is her, and then — this happens very quickly — we're face to face, I would like to give her a kiss, but just at that moment I drop from where I've been hovering in the sky, and I'm falling to the earth so fast my eyes are forced shut and the wind is screaming like a runaway train and . . . it makes my head hurt, like I said. Like I think I said, the idea of home.

∽

I think I will lie down again and try to get some sleep. It's almost five in the morning. I can see now how the sun might rise. Often in the darkest middle part of the night it seems impossible. But at this hour there are signs. I'm very tired, too tired to soak my feet as I had planned, too tired to undress, too tired to check on Hercules, too tired to think of the call, too tired even to crawl under my blanket.

It is 6:12 a.m. I've been dreaming of a 1948 Oldsmobile. I'm sitting next to Elvira. She's fifteen years old and driving her dad's car without a licence. Now I'm not so sure it was a dream. I think it is a memory and that in fact I haven't been sleeping at all. I'm sorely tempted to get up and look out my window to see if perhaps there's a '48 Olds idling in the parking lot, ready to take me away from here. Elvira and I and several of our friends had borrowed her dad's car for a trip to Winnipeg. She and I shared a bag of sunflower seeds and just for dumheit she drove home from the city through the dry ditches of the countryside instead of on the Trans-Canada Highway. That big Olds handled the culverts well. Our friends were in the back seat, and we all had a terrific time! Until the police stopped us and confiscated her father's car and threatened us with farm labour, which is what juvenile delinquents did in my day. I mentioned to the police officer that I was up to my neck in farm labour at the present, which made my friends smile anyway. I felt the sting of his knuckled backhand across my face.

Elvira leapt into the fray and shouted at the police officer, How dare you, or How could you, or something along those lines. She and I weren't dating at that point, but it was at that moment following her defiant outburst that I fell in love with her. And furthermore I realized that I would need a girl like her if I were to survive. At the time, however, it wasn't so much a conscious realization, but more of an instinct.

Seeing as the car was confiscated anyway, we spent the rest of the day bowling and in the evening we all split the cost of a cab back to Steinbach (forty miles). I sat next to Elvira in the back seat, and my legs shook so badly from nervousness that they knocked over the bag of sunflower seeds she had balanced in her lap and I spent the rest of the drive home picking seeds off the floor of the cab, apologizing intermittently, and shaking.

Unfortunately, I have tracked blood all over the floor of my room. My blisters have opened up again and I'm not sure what to use to wipe it up. A nurse will enter soon and sigh. Have placed several sheets of notepad paper on the floor to soak up the blood. Have placed my feet in the large blue container beside my bed. Will wait for nurse.

❧

Once, after Elvira and I had started dating, I borrowed her father's car to pick her up in the city. I parked it in front of her dormitory (she was in nurses' training. How I wish I were her patient now!) and went inside to meet her. She wasn't in her room, however, and when I returned to the spot where I had parked the car, it was gone! This was the brand-new 1952 Oldsmobile of the man I had hoped would become my father-in-law. I ran wildly up and down the street in search of the car, berating myself for being such a country bumpkin as to leave the keys in the ignition, plotting my own mysterious disappearance, imagining the inevitable break-up between Elvira and me, bracing myself against my mother's icy disapproval and my own abject shame, calculating the number of chicken heads I'd have to hack off for my father in order to make enough money to buy another 1952 Olds, when who should drive past as casually as can be, elbow sticking out of the window and a bright yellow scarf tied up around her shiny black hair, but Elvira. It took her a good half an hour before she could speak without erupting into raucous gales of laughter.

I agreed with her, eventually, that it had been an excellent practical joke, and even conceded to having the story told, in detail, to her girlfriends back at the dormitory, to her brothers back in town, to her father, who enjoyed it immensely, and to all of our friends.

I've decided to go for a walk! Have just realized in the same instant that my feet are bleeding. Never mind, I'll try. The nurse came in and asked me what I was doing. I said I was going for a walk and I'd be back in time for breakfast. She gave me some pills and asked me to wait for a few minutes while she "cleared it." Rather kind of her to play this game with me, I think. Pills taking effect, no walk.

⁓

It is 6:46 a.m. I have been unable to move. I did not go out as planned. I had hoped this wouldn't happen. My optimism soars to such a peak that just as suddenly it plummets off the edge. The edge of . . . that place where optimism plummets. (I'm sorry.) I'm trying to be precise. I'm trying to write down the facts. Perhaps if I rest briefly . . . it's still quite early. More later . . .

It is now 7:32. I'm afraid that if I give in to sleep there will be no end. I'll have wasted this opportunity to clarify things. I'll have failed. I will force myself to begin again.

I recall a day. A large sparrow blocked the small entrance of the birdhouse I had built for a family of wrens. The sparrow was too big to get through the hole. My daughter Miriam (she was five or six) and I stood at the kitchen window and looked at the sparrow. Inside the birdhouse, we knew, were six or seven baby birds waiting hungrily for their mother to return with food. The sparrow, by blocking the entrance, was preventing the mother wren from returning home to feed her babies. We watched as the mother wren flew over the birdhouse, around and around, unable to land.

But why? asked Miriam. What good does it do the sparrow? I didn't know either, and not knowing bothered me. I had assumed until that day that it was the circumstantial misery of human beings that made us enjoy the suffering of others. Or if not enjoy, exactly, then stand complacently by and allow it to happen. But if birds did it too, I thought, then perhaps it was a baser instinct that arose naturally from all life. This thought depressed me horribly. I felt there was no hope for the world, that evil would inevitably triumph over good, and that there was, therefore, no point in striving for goodness. And yet I also felt that the struggle to be good was the purpose of life. Certainly of my life.

But never mind. Elvira, at the precise moment of what my older daughter at the time would have called my existential crisis, came to join my younger daughter and me at the window. What's so interesting out there? she asked. We told her and in a flash she had grabbed a broom, run into the backyard, and shooed that sparrow away. The mother wren quickly flew into the birdhouse and, presumably, all was well again. Elvira came inside and told us, my daughter and me, that if the sparrow returned, we should simply do what she had done and foadich met de zach (a Low German expression meaning "be done with it"). Then, as though nothing significant had occurred, she cheerfully began to make supper.

Shoo the sparrow away and get on with supper. This is the first part of my new life strategy. Will worry less. I hope I don't ask my next visitor for a broom, as a form of greeting. Why can't I say hello, simply? I'm forgetting the basics. My brother popped in for a cameo a few minutes ago and said, How's my big brother? and I said, pointing to the brochure, Those houses are all facing east, why do you think that is? It's hard to backtrack after that. I mean hello, I'm fine, yourself? How goes the business of running hospitals in rural Manitoba? My feet keep bleeding, I don't know why. That sort of thing. The wife and kids.

∽

Well, the day has definitely begun. I hear the vacuum cleaner approaching from down the hall, and I imagine that the maid, or not the maid, and I will go through some type of scenario in which she offers to clean my room and I politely decline the offer. I can't let her see the blood. In the meantime I absolutely must mobilize the troops and begin!

I have just remembered my money problems. I am down to $141. How will I pay for this room? How will I remove the stains from the floor? I am beginning to panic, but not terribly so.

Sure enough, the maid is cross with me. You gotta have your room cleaned and re-towelled sometime, she hollered at me from outside the door. Why, I asked her, why must I? Because it's my job, she said. Yes, but if I'm happy with things exactly the way they are, then why must you clean? Why must I have fresh towels? You don't understand, she said, you don't get it.

Fair enough, I answered, but I don't need clean towels. Thank you and good luck. Why I wished her good luck I haven't a clue. The nurse came in then and apologized to the maid for me. This is not a hotel, Mel, she said kindly. We have to clean your room.

Very well. Jarring, mind you, but not the end of the world. I don't know why I'm so reluctant to have the maid clean my room. I'd prefer a harmonious relationship with her, there's no doubt of that. In any case, I can't have her discovering the bloodstains on the floor, and now, as well, the paper I used to soak it up is ruined. Must remind daughter to bring more. And pens.

I can no longer make out the sound of the vacuum cleaner. She must have gone to another floor. I will make a sign for my doorknob that reads: C'mon in, patient is already disturbed.

✐

I'll just spend a few minutes looking out my window at my late brother-in-law's house, directly across the street from the hospital. Births of family members in this hospital: My parents, Elvira's parents, all of their children including Elvira and myself, our daughters. Deaths of family members in this hospital: Elvira's parents, my parents, Elvira's brother, who used to live across the street. His wife still does. I'm looking at her house. She has come to visit me many times. She is an angel, truly. (Will not tell me the truth about E.) On one of these visits I told her I had seen George in the corridor. No, no, honey, she said in Low German, George died several years ago. Don't you remember? You wrote the obituary. Yes! I said, grateful to her for having reminded me, and he always wanted it longer. That's right, sweetie, she said, that's right. Occurred to me that he had wanted to make love to her one last time before dying. Almost made the mistake of asking her if he had.

What I have seen: sunshine, house, trees, car, pavement, fountain.

I have always enjoyed the sun's warmth and I feel, as I write this, that the sun is the last reminder of my good life on Earth. This is so ridiculous as to be embarrassing, but I feel as though the sun were my friend! Do you remember those books we used to read when we were very small? Where the young protagonists enjoy close imaginary relationships with planets and stars to the point where they are greeting them by name and, in their minds, bringing them into their homes and telling them their deepest secrets, hopes, and dreams?

That's how I feel! The sunlight makes me feel at home, as though I own it, that it's mine exclusively, that I've invented it, or that it's a member of my family. The sun helps me remember the good times, and in remembering the good times I can then safely say that in fact I've had good times. How's that for my next non-greeting to visitor: In fact, I've had good times! or how about, The sun is my friend! (Is there no activity room in this place? Ping-pong or something?) I've begun to count the beats between my greetings and my visitors' replies. Number of beats that passed between my last greeting of "I said I didn't need any more towels" and visitor's reply of "I didn't bring towels, Mel": four.

∽

A construction site is barely visible (is it the housing development?) through my window and I have watched the men at work, marvelling at the level of skill and cooperation such a large-scale venture must require. I remember the house we built on First Street, a solid project, a cozy home for Elvira and me to begin . . . to begin.

In my files you'll find old black-and-white photographs with serrated edges that capture the work in progress, the building of the house, from empty lot to finished product. A wide grin on my face, a nail in the corner of my mouth, a hammer in my hand, proud and slightly overwhelmed by the turn my life has taken, new wife, new home, baby on the way, and a job I love. In the evening my students would stroll past the house in progress and invariably lend a hand for an hour or two. In this photograph I weigh only a hundred and forty pounds, drowning in an oversized lumber jacket and wool cap, flaps and all, Elvira in a nightie, also smiling from ear to ear, her dark hair a little messy, the morning sun pouring in through the windows of our brand-new kitchen. Elvira is wearing the First Nightgown! Every year I bought her a nightgown for Christmas, some sheer and flimsy, others prim and flannelly, depending, I suppose, on my mood at the time of purchase. Okay, where's my new nightie, Mel? she would ask as we sat around the tree opening gifts. It became a tradition for Elvira to parade around our house on Christmas Eve in her new nightie as the girls and I looked on admiringly.

In the photograph we appear, almost, to have been taken by surprise, and years later she and I would try to remember who the photographer was and whether he or she had caught us off guard, or whether surprise was simply a permanent expression on our faces in those early years when so much was new.

One May evening a student of mine got caught in the rain on his way home from a softball game. He knocked on our door, drenched and dripping, wondering if he might come in out of the rain. Of course we invited him inside, even though we were both in our housecoats and ready for bed, and Elvira offered to dry his clothes in her new dryer. What would he wear in the meantime? he asked. Elvira rushed off to our bedroom and brought out one of my suits.

This student of mine was big for his eleven years, tall and stocky, and my suit fit him to a T! Oh, how Elvira laughed and laughed as I stood next to this boy trying to explain concepts of long division. Eventually she left the room but the boy and I could hear her muffled laughter from the kitchen and we exchanged nervous looks. Later, after the boy had gone home in his own clothes, I asked Elvira why she had laughed so hard, and she told me, through fresh laughter, that the boy, in my suit, looked as old as I, and that I, in my housecoat, looked like an eleven-year-old boy.

For some reason I took exception to this (oh, for that to be my biggest beef now) and remained silent for a time until at last, around midnight, I said to her, Well, you're young looking yourself, you know. And wouldn't you know, this set her off again. I was concerned that the neighbours would be awoken by Elvira's laughter. I leapt from the bed and closed the window and begged her to stop laughing. She wouldn't though and insisted that I begin laughing, until eventually I did emit a chuckle or two and the two of us went to bed happy. We were young, twenty-one years old, learning how to live with one another, and filled with wonder.

Filleted with wonder. Wonder-filled. I'd like to apologize to someone for killing my wife. (Wife would be first choice, but of course wouldn't mean much.) Will wait for opportunity. In the meantime . . .

✐

Complete the following story:

"It was February 10, 1888. The prairie wind howled over the snow waves outside our small log-mud house. It was Saturday, and there was going to be a social in town. I wondered how difficult that ten-mile journey was going to be, but I really wanted to go. Sarah would be there and . . ."

One of my favourite assignments from the section "The Pioneering Experience in Western Canada After 1867 (Rural and Urban)." When I came up with it, I was only nineteen, fresh out of normal school and barely an adult myself. I changed the name from Elvira to Sarah and presto, an assignment my students can enjoy writing and I can enjoy reading. Of course, in grade six the girls were usually imagining that Sarah was their best friend and the boys that she was their older sister and that it wasn't fair that Sarah could go to the social and they couldn't. My students have provided me with more than a thousand versions of endings to this opening paragraph, the oddest having to do with a young woman named Sarah who poses by day as a Mennonite pioneer and by night as a wildly popular dancer and who makes a ten-mile trek to see her seem like two. Well, anyway . . . (Loud crash in corridor: nurse curses in Low German, Deusant! meaning "thousand," as in a thousand curses. Shocking.)

Of course not everything about teaching school was idyllic. I had the odd parent who would call me up in a rage if their child had failed a test or received a low mark, or if the child had been bullied and I had failed to notice. I've had a parent threaten to tar and feather me if I didn't pass his daughter into the next grade, back in the days when students could be kept back. My living-room window has been shot at with a pellet gun. I had one mother who was furious about another student accidentally spilling ink on her son's pants. She screamed into the telephone, in Low German, asking me why I didn't teach my students to be more careful, what was I going to do about her son's pants, and how would I make sure it never happened again. I assured her that I would remind my students to be more careful in the future, but she continued to holler. I told her I'd have my wife launder his pants (this was the fifties and I hadn't used a washing machine ever. Still haven't, mind you) but that wasn't good enough either. I told her I'd reimburse her for her son's pants, but nothing I said could appease her and she continued to scream at me over the phone. Finally I lost my cool. Elvira remembers this occasion as one of the few times I've defended myself, the other being with her brother Edward, who needed me to remind him that teachers work hard too, even if the pay isn't spectacular. Anyway, I'd had enough with this irate mother and I interrupted her rant in a loud voice and said, in Low German: I don't tell you how much salt to put on your potatoes and you don't tell me how to teach school! And then I hung up!

I can't remember a time before or since that I've hung up on a person, although I've dearly wanted to. That was the end of the ink incident, thankfully. I do regret not having given her the money for a new pair of pants for her son, because I can see now that her rage was born from desperate poverty, and that for her, a recent Paraguayan Mennonite immigrant, the purchase of a new pair of pants would have been an enormous expense, and that if the pants, very likely the boy's only pair, hadn't been replaced, he would have worn them and felt humiliated by the stains. I can't remember if he got a new pair or not, but I hope so, and I wish I had paid for them.

6

Declarations of love and regret: I have read this in a newspaper article re the unfortunate men and women on death row in the United States. The article quoted a prison warden who, with this sentence (fragment), described the typical last words of those condemned to die. The prison chaplain is also quoted. He says that most men and women on death row find God in their final months, as did the men in the fox trenches of wartime.

Why do we wait, I wonder, until we're caught? Do we mean it finally, that we believe? Or are we scared? If we believed, would we be scared? Is this what is meant by the fear of God? Are we saying please help me now and comfort me? I haven't needed you till now but deusant! I've seen the error of my ways and perhaps I needed you all along but pretended not to and now I want to make up for it. It happens, doesn't it, that we find ourselves praying in tense situations.

And do we do the same with loved ones? With parents and children and brothers and sisters? Towards the end when things become clear . . . we do, don't we? Declarations of love and regret. We're no different, in the end, than the prisoners on death row, except that we feel we have lots of time for declarations later. I mean, I'm not alone, am I?

C.S. Lewis, one of my favourite writers, said that we read to know we're not alone. I'm . . . There's a person here. Person has left. Knows me, but I haven't a clue who he is. Have lost train of thought. Wonder how I greeted him. Can only imagine. Forgot to count the beats.

I have always wanted to write a book about the life of my friend Henry. He has had a fascinating life, as a young boy fleeing with the other Mennonites from the Russian soldiers, witnessing the death of his grandmother along the way, at the age of ten, making his way to Germany and finally to Canada. Today he is a jovial man who hates to lose at cards. Well, that makes sense, doesn't it? One day, several years ago, he and I and our wives drove to the town of Souris. I asked him if he'd be brave enough to ride a bike across the Souris swinging bridge, the longest of its kind in North America. Of course, he said, but I don't have a bike. I asked one of the local boys who was hanging around the bridge if Henry could borrow his bike and ride it across the bridge, which is only about two feet wide, quite bouncy, and fenced in with some flimsy rope. Sure, said the boy, and off went Henry! At the age of sixty-two! I enjoyed that man's company. Am beginning to suspect he was here moments ago. That he was the visitor. Would explain why he came to mind. Hope he returns.

All my life I have read biographies of famous men and women, mostly politicians and journalists, and these life stories help to give my own a little context, and also inspiration. They give me tips on living, goals to strive for, pitfalls to avoid, they teach me about life. I look up to these individuals. I suppose that sounds boyish but it's the truth.

We read to know we're not alone. C.S. Lewis was a brilliant

man in my opinion. He believed in God, he was a good writer, and a kind person by all accounts. One question I would have liked to ask him, however, is this: how does a man feel less alone when he can no longer read?

Some faith in words, but not all. Where to turn when words stop making sense? The book on Henry won't get written, after all, at least not by me. So what's left? Declarations of love and regret? Arsenals of medication? Popsicle sticks and pipe cleaners?

⸺

Lined paper, unlined paper, stiff recipe cards, notebooks, notepads, Post-Its, paper, paper, paper. All blank. These were the gifts I gave my daughters and not much else, I'm afraid. I have neglected them horribly and it's much too late now to make amends. They tell me in big block letters that I have not neglected them, that I have provided them with everything they could ever want in life, with holidays and riding lessons and music lessons and summer camp and new bicycles and a cottage at the lake and university and . . . They tell me I was a good father, but they of course are lying to me, trying to make me feel better. Oh no, I say, that's not enough. Then they tell me I was no different from any father of my generation in this town. Fathers worked, they say, period, that's how it was. They cite examples. Write it down, please, I ask them, and they do. (Needn't be in big block letters, I don't say.)

I have pages and pages of YOU'RE A GOOD FATHER, A GOOD MAN, AND WE ARE PROUD OF YOU. THIS IS NOT YOUR FAULT. WE LOVE YOU AND WE KNOW YOU LOVE US. Please write it down one more time, I ask them, and they do. I have vowed to be honest with daughters the next time I see them and break it to them that I'm able to decipher cursive.

You should have seen my face light up when my daughter

brought these notepads in to the hospital, along with a package of Bic ballpoint pens. I tried to write down what I thought were the pertinent points. I often asked her to repeat them. First and foremost on my mind was when I was going to be reunited with Elvira. Soon, she said, very soon. And twenty seconds later I'd ask again. I wrote it all down as best I could. I reminded myself of phone calls I needed to make, questions I needed to ask, but towards the end I was going in circles. Towards the end I was going in circles. Towards the end I asked her to write it down for me.

When I was a boy I fell out of a crabapple tree and broke my arm. My mother had three words for me: Can you write? For some odd reason, I cherish that moment. I have never felt closer to her, before or since, except for maybe when she added "ice cubes" to what not to give the baby. Baby, now grown, due to arrive for visit soon. Will try to tell him what he wants to hear. He talks about Mother. He compares my reluctance to discuss my problems to Mother's own inability to admit to her drinking problem. This comparison horrifies me. Mentally, I make a note of the differences between Mother and me. Oddly, I focus on this detail: that Mother once sold Elvira an old copy of her *Reader's Digest* magazine for twenty-five cents after Elvira had expressed some interest in one of its articles. I recall how intensely ashamed I was of Mother's pettiness. I tell myself that I am generous with money. There are, of course, more relevant differences, but I cannot seem to move away, in my mind, from this *Reader's Digest* incident.

My mother was an interesting woman. She attended church regularly, same pew, different hats, was always well dressed, disapproved of drinking, was an avowed teetotaller, wrote a gossip column called "Pot Pourri" for the town paper for more than forty years, and, from time to time, stole bottles of vanilla from Economy Foods and drank herself into a stupor. At various intervals the manager of Economy Foods would tally up the cost of all the bottles she had shoplifted and I would write him a cheque. This is a typical small-town agreement having to do with the preservation of dignity. Or it is a means of not rocking the boat, a lie. An arrangement available to those with money and status, and not to the general alcoholic public.

When my father was alive and my mother had been drinking (she began at the age of seventeen), he would cry. He didn't know what to do or where to turn. Mrs. I.Q. Unger, before she died, told me my father would sit at her kitchen table and cry like a baby, sick with grief over my mother's drinking. Perhaps she should have been confronted by the manager, by the police, thrown in jail and publicly shamed. But that's not how it was done. Over the years Elvira tried to get her to talk about her drinking. She tried to pinpoint some underlying problems that may have caused it. She tried to exorcise her demons. I, of course, said nothing. Elvira encouraged her to attend the local Alcoholics Anonymous meetings. But my mother refused to admit she drank. How many times did I let myself into her apartment to find her stumbling about, bruised and rambling? I've lost count.

As I clean her up, wash the floor, fetch a new housedress from the closet, throw away the bottles, and disinfect her fresh cuts, I listen to her talk about my brother, Reg, who is very busy in the United States establishing a reputation that will, some day, give him the credentials he needs to take charge of mental health care in the province and, finally, to manage hospitals, like this one.

And I listen to her talk about Diana, who is a missionary in Central America. My mother misses her children. And what will you do with your life, Melvin? she asks me as I gather up her soiled clothes and put them in a plastic bag, which I will give to Elvira to launder. I don't talk about it. We don't talk about it. Elvira talks about it, but I don't talk about it.

We are worried, my daughter said, we are worried about him. He is becoming more agitated, more confused, manic. Will you make sure he isn't discharged? There's nobody at the house. Mom is in the city, she can't . . . she needs to rest. It's very important that he stays here, although he will tell you he is fine and he will be convincing. Please don't let him leave.

You have our word.

Words again. More words. I told them I would be fine and they believed me. I said the words and they believed me. They let me leave.

Reg? Are you there? Aren't you going to tell me it's time to stop running and come home?

December 28, 1956. Our wedding day, and night, but what a personal fiasco that was on my part. Too nervous, suffice to say, and Elvira as calm as you can please, eventually falling fast asleep while I fidgeted next to her, not believing my luck in one second and in the next furious with myself for my inability to perform. My wedding-night grade? A resounding F! But here's a historic point of interest: our wedding night cost me eleven dollars. Naturally I have kept the receipt. And the room in the hotel in which our wedding photographs were taken is now a beautiful round cocktail lounge with a high marble ceiling and a live piano player.

And now a leap: Elvira's pregnancy. (You can rightly assume that I finally adjusted to my newfound marital status and became more assured of my conjugal responsibilities, of myself as husband.) Elvira became pregnant with our first daughter sometime — she would remember exactly when — in September, and it doesn't surprise me that conception occurred in that month. I would have been feeling happiest and most relaxed, of course, because I would have only just embarked upon a new school year, and that was traditionally a time when my hopes and my energy level were high. Come to think of it, Elvira might have been feeling most relaxed at that time as well, with me safely out from underfoot as I had been all summer.

When, at Christmastime, Elvira felt enough time had passed and the "danger period" was over, she decided she would share our happy news with the neighbours. The reaction of our next-door neighbour lady ("neighbour lady" is a term I've always been fond of) was: I've known you were pregnant for ages, Elvira, because you haven't been opening your curtains first thing in the morning. Now that's small-town living! Elvira, of course, was vomiting first thing in the morning, while the curtains stayed shut for an extra ten minutes.

When my second daughter, also conceived in that fresh, exciting month of September when real work resumed, was born, the neighbour ladies, this time all of them — not to mention the men and women I taught school with — knew almost immediately that Elvira had had her baby. How? Marjorie, a mere six-year-old, had gone to school resplendent in white knee socks and a white cotton dress, but missing the red and blue sash that was meant to go around the waist and be tied in a big festive bow at the back. Now who but a novice, somebody who had never dressed a child in his life, would forget an accessory as vital to an ensemble as a sash? And why was that incompetent fumbler dressing this child in the first place? Obviously the child's mother was away, and where would she be? That's right, in the hospital having another.

It's nearly impossible to break news in a small town. Some might say that's part of a small town's charm, and some might not.

❧

Just remembered something that might explain why, on top of everything else, I was so nervous on my wedding night. It has to do with the small fire that occurred earlier in the day at the church, during the part of the wedding ceremony where Elvira and I signed our names in the registry.

As Elvira leaned over, next to a burning candelabra, pen in hand and all smiles, her veil, carelessly flung back by yours truly when the minister allowed us to kiss, grazed the tip of the candle and burst into flame.

Before you could say Jack be nimble, Jack be quick, Elvira's friend Kathy had leapt from her position as maid of honour, yanked the fiery veil from Elvira's head, flung it to the floor, and, as though participating in some tribal wedding ritual known only to Russian Mennonites, hiked up her skirts and lace roundabouts and stomped on the fire until every living ember had seen its last.

Then — and at this point I was still scarcely aware of the events taking place — her sister Wilma turned and lit right out of the church, hightailing it all the way to her house on Ash Street (that's not a joke), where she grabbed her own wedding veil from its storage box in the basement. Then, with seconds to go before the organist was scheduled to begin the "Wedding March" and Elvira and I were to parade jubilantly down the aisle to our waiting hansom, she flew into the church, rammed the lacy thing onto Elvira's bare head, and, as demurely as she could, stepped back into line, next to the best man, who looked like he was about to faint, and nodded at Elvira as if to say, Carry on, little sister, everything's under control.

Elvira thought it was a terribly funny thing to have happen at a wedding, but I did not. I was of the school that believed weddings were not a time for terribly funny things, and I blamed myself for not taking better care of my new bride. If I had known better, I would have arranged the registry and the candelabra differently. For years after I would imagine safer arrangements of these items and conjure up in my mind more appropriate endings to the wedding we had rehearsed, at my insistence, so many times. Elvira, after only ten minutes or so into our first rehearsal, clapped her hands together, grabbed her coat, and said, Well, that'll be great, let's go!

That fire bothered me more than I ever let on, and as Elvira recounted the tale, in all its hilarious detail, to whoever would listen, I would sit quietly, smiling at intervals and waiting for it to be over. I couldn't quite stop believing that somehow it was my failure, even though Elvira would have thought it was ridiculous for me to think so.

Have just eaten lunch while listening to a conversation two nurses were having in the hallway outside my room re Hercules. He will soon be going home is the gist of it. I will miss him. Nurse asked me casually, What are you writing? My answer: What am I writing? Almost made the mistake of drinking a container of tube-feeding liquid left out on my tray, bound for another room. Thought it was a box of Boost.

Have read in the paper about a postal worker who was fired for homelessness. He refused to give up his government-issued uniform because as long as he wore it he could ride the bus at no cost, according to policy. He carried the mailbag with him at all times too, stuffed full with his belongings. And so, because he lived on the streets, he became scruffier and scruffier, until finally his uniform became so soiled and tattered that it was unrecognizable as a letter carrier's outfit and the bus drivers stopped letting him ride for free. Now he walks along his former mail route every day, dressed in rags. The letter carrier currently delivering the mail in that area doesn't mind if this chap joins him as long as he doesn't step onto private property or handle any of the mail.

I mentioned this story to a nurse a while ago and she informed me that the world is full of oddballs.

Perhaps I should go for a little walk. Though a little walk, or should I say a short walk, may be next to impossible considering my propensity for marathon hikes, but we shall see. Naturally I don't want to miss my call, but I must weigh the urgency of receiving the call with the urgency of my need for fresh air, and hope for the best.

∽

I'm back after having gotten as far as the front doors. I forgot to factor in the urgency of the nurses' need to know where I'm going. I had no answer. I've been foiled. Makes me want to scream. I never scream. Must relax.

Now I am recalling Marj's youthful face at fifteen, how she so resembled Elvira, and now a hotel room where we all spent the night, the family on vacation, a few tiffs perhaps between the girls, my snoring, of course, a problem, some engine trouble in South Dakota, but otherwise thoroughly enjoyable. And Elvira so very happy to be away from town for a while, never wanting to return. I remember holidays more clearly than home life. I was happy too, it would seem, away from the town. And yet always relieved to have returned, unlike Elvira, who'd rather travel forever . . . another road trip, piles of Wrigley's chewing gum wrappers beside me on the car seat, the girls dividing them up to make necklaces, Elvira reading a whodunit, bare feet on the dashboard . . . Judy Garland's real name is Frances Gumm, the girls tell me. What would you change your name to if you could, Dad? Hank Aaron, I tell them.

Those days of misplaced shaving kits were happy times. If my shaving kit was lost, it meant we were together as a family, away somewhere, either at the cottage or on a road trip. Perhaps I intentionally misplaced my shaving kit, a brown leather zippered deal with a looped strap, as a sort of guaranteed shtick that would make the girls laugh.

Even now my shaving habits are big news with all sorts of people. Today he shaved! No, he hasn't shaved in weeks. Has he shaved this morning? Encourage him to shave. He won't shave. He shaved!

Which reminds me of a recent visit to the doctor. I was, of course, how couldn't I be, aware of the profound significance of my shaven or unshaven face. I knew that the occasion of a doctor's appointment necessitated the act of shaving. (Have you shaved? Have you washed? Have you eaten? Have you run the Boston Marathon?) It was only after the appointment, as I stood at the bathroom sink, razor in hand, gazing sadly at my foamy reflection, that Elvira gently reminded me of the sequence. Mel, she said in a soft whisper all empty of hope, you might have shaved before the appointment.

✐

A nurse has entered my room. She is my least favourite nurse and I have decided that I will continue to write while she fiddles around with things rather than do my usual smiling and chatting. She is looking at my feet as I write. She has just said, Mr. Toews, why won't you stay off your feet? Why don't you call us when your blisters open? I am not answering. Mr. Toews, she says in a loud, impatient voice, I'm talking to you! I am not going to stop writing. Mr. Toews! Put down your notepad and look at me!

I noticed, in my youth, that the women of my community could easily be identified as Bergthalers or Chortitzer or E.M.C.

or M.B. or E.M.B. or Kleinegemeinde or Schrodenfitzer depending on their hair. Chortitzers wore wraps or nets over their heads, and they were considered very conservative; Kleinegemeinde women had tight shiny rolls along the edges of their hair, less conservative; and M.B.ers wore all-purpose buns. Landmark women, on the other hand, never wear wraps, nets, rolls, or buns. They have wild uncombed hair that sprays out from the head at all angles, wispy and tangled, and rather alluring in an alarming unconventional way. Landmark women remain a mystery to me, although Elvira befriended one or two of them in her younger days. Once I asked Elvira about the Landmark hairdo and she said, Oh, they have less time to deal with it. Which made me wonder what they do over there in Landmark, Manitoba.

I believe there is an extremely conservative Mennonite church near Landmark called the Sommerfeld Church, where singing in harmony is not allowed. Perhaps that's changed. Or is it the church in Lowe Farm? At any rate, the singing is, of course, unaccompanied by piano or organ. (Instruments are worldly.) There is a group of men who lead the congregation in song. They are called the ferzinge, the front singers, or the lead singers. They will set the key and begin to sing, and the congregation will follow half a note behind. At times the ferzinge will stop and start again if the congregation is not in the right key. Wada aunfange, they will say. From the top!

The nurse is rebandaging my feet now, muttering as she does so about my lack of cooperation and how hard it is for her to do her job with patients like me. I haven't looked up from my notebook, and I'm desperate for something to write, I can't let my pen stop, or have her think I'm only scribbling, and so . . .

Speaking of school days, I shamefully recall the day I stabbed Elvira with the sharp end of my compass. I suppose I was seven or eight and just beginning to have feelings,

unknowable, inexpressible feelings, of . . . love? No. Infatuation?
I'm not sure, even today, what you would call that vague need
for approval from the opposite sex. In any case, I wanted
Elvira to like me, and in my mind though not consciously at
the time, I thought I could spur that approval on by . . . stabbing her? No, not the actual stabbing, but the display of nerve
and timing and discernment (I chose her, after all) that the
stabbing act required (I got her in the rear end as she walked
past my desk). Let me explain before I go on that stabbing is
really too strong a word: no blood was drawn, no stitches
required, no charges laid, and I certainly yanked my hand back
immediately after my compass made the slightest contact.
Elvira said, Ouch! and hit me, and I was made to stand
between the sink and the waste paper basket with my face to
the wall.

But this, of course, started something between the two of
us, even though it was a mixture of hostility and disdain on
Elvira's part. I was thrilled. I had been noticed! This act of so-
called love and bravery was quite a remarkable achievement
for a shy boy like me, at least I thought so. Elvira was the feisty
one, after all. (She began school at age two because she was
tired of sitting around at home all day, although she was made
to repeat kindergarten three times until the rest of her peers
could catch up to her.)

Somewhere in my collection there is a school photograph of
our kindergarten class. Elvira is wearing a short brown dress,
thick knit stockings, sturdy leather shoes, and, unfortunately,
two fierce braids (I loathe braids) and is sitting on the grass in
the front row with her legs spread, her elbows out like two
handles on a teacup, her neck craned forward and her face jut-
ting towards the camera. She is taking up far too much room
(in the photo her head is twice the size of everybody else's),
and the girls on either side of her are squished in and trying to
hold their own for the shot. She has that expression on her

face that seems to say, I've just done something extremely naughty and I'm as pleased as punch about it.

I, on the other hand, am standing nicely and sedately and unobtrusively (this photo was taken two years before the compass incident) in the back row, just to the left of Elvira. My short blond hair is wedged firmly over to one side with the help of my mother's spit and I am wearing a smart beige sweater with two wide horizontal stripes. I'm smiling, slightly, and nervous. Elvira and I were to be classmates virtually for the rest of our school days.

⁓

Nurse still here. Still muttering. Must think quickly of something to write. If she dares to take my notebook away from me I'll hit her. No, no I won't. I don't know what I'll do. Keep writing.

⁓

For some reason I recall a conversation Elvira and I had a few years ago. We were driving home from the city, and it was snowing.

How do you feel? she asked me. Well, it's different, I said.

We were quiet for a minute or two.

In what way is it different? she asked me.

Well, I said after a lengthy pause, it's not the same.

Mel, she said finally, you teach language arts. You teach children how to write. I haven't heard you use a "feeling" word.

We smiled. I enjoyed her teasing. We were quiet for another minute or two.

Are you sad? she asked, knowing.

I don't know what point I'm trying to make. It's just a recollection and I can't quite remember what we were talking

about, what was different and making me sad. I suppose . . .
No, I don't know. But why didn't I say more? For a man who
loves words, why can't I speak? Why don't I talk? What will I
talk about? Myself? I probably haven't said the right things, or
the things, in any case, that help to explain who I am. I haven't
talked about myself. Is that ungenerous or self-effacing? Is it
bad or is it good? What comes from talking about oneself? Is
there a reason for it? Have I withheld words in anger? And if
so, who am I punishing with my silence? And why? Or is it the
Depression that lodges its evil self within my throat and blocks
my speech? Is depression anger? And if so, what am I angry
about? Can anger cause a chemical imbalance in the brain
(because that is what depression is generally regarded as being
these days)? One talks (if one isn't me) to one's psychiatrist for
approximately fifty minutes, and then is given a prescription
for a drug that will, with any luck, make all the talk, the talk of
sadness and hopelessness, unnecessary. Eventually, the talking
becomes a kind of scripted warm-up exercise, a quick prelude
to the real cure, the drug. The talking becomes a means to a
better end, that is, the elimination of the need to talk. Doctors
are very busy individuals, after all, and a prescription requires
less than a minute of one's time. I should add, however, that I
was without a doubt one of the least cooperative psychiatric
patients on my doctor's roster (we're quite a team), not that I
behaved like Jack Nicholson in *One Flew Over the Cuckoo's
Nest* (I didn't get the hype) but because I was consistently
pleasant and upbeat. And dishonest. Everything is fine, I
assured my doctors, just fine. This was one of the reasons that
Elvira had such a difficult time convincing doctors that everything was not fine. That's why she became so tired. Nobody
believed her because I lied and said everything was fine when
it wasn't. It's how I killed her.

⤳

Mr. Toews! It is time for your medication. You'll have to stop writing . . . Mr. Toews!

Go back to the beginning, Mel, write it all down, write anything, anything at all. I love . . . No, not that, write down what you remember. A new life strategy? No, no, too late for that. Go back and start again, and this time be honest.

The story of my grandfather, the youngest person in the group of Mennonites that came over, in 1874, to Canada from Russia. Queen Victoria saw to it that we Mennonites would be given free farmland in the Prairies, and the Canadian government assured us that we'd be able to live the way we wanted to, apart from the world. His is a very romantic tale of shunning (Mennonite policy of ensuring sinner feels ashamed) and elopement that begins, sadly, with a death.

My grandfather and my grandmother were a happy young couple way back in the early 1900s. He farmed and she kept house. In short order, while still in their twenties, four children were born, my father, Henry, being the second. My grandmother would complain from time to time of headaches, but naturally there wasn't much she could do for them other than rest, and with four little children and a multitude of household chores unheard of today, rest was at a premium.

One day, while preparing a noon meal for her family, my

grandmother fell to the floor and died. Later it was determined that she was the victim of a brain aneurysm. Or perhaps, at that time, it was thought that she had a blood clot in her brain. My grandfather, still a young man, was left to raise the four young children on his own, in addition to his full-time farm work. As I recall, the youngest of the four children, a baby named Abe, after his father, Abraham, was soon moved into his grandparents' home, where he remained permanently and became known in the community as Groutfodasch Abe, or "Grandparents' Abe." Every Sunday, my grandfather and the other children would go to my grandfather's in-laws' home for a good meal and a visit with Groutfodasch Abe.

During the day the three remaining children would tumble along behind my grandfather in the field, or ride two or three at a time on top of the plowhorse, while my grandfather did his best to prevent them from being injured. Late in the evening, they would all return to the (increasingly untidy) farmhouse, and my grandfather would cook a large meal of fried eggs. According to the story told to me, it was always fried eggs.

Occasionally his sisters or one or two ladies from the church would take pity on my grandfather and bring a hot meal of something other than eggs to the house or offer to do the laundry or wash the floors or the children or both. Over the years, however, it became clear that my grandfather would need regular help in the home and with the children, especially during the seeding and harvesting seasons, which found him out on the fields virtually day and night. He had during this time attempted to court a fine young woman from down the road, but alas, she had turned him down.

After mulling it over a bit with his sisters, it was agreed that my grandfather would "hire a girl" to help him. In exchange for room and board (and all the eggs she could eat) this girl would keep house and mind the children. Word quickly got out that Grandfather was looking for a housekeeper, and in no time a seventeen-year-old Holdeman (an extremely conservative sect of Mennonites) girl was hired by committee (the sisters) and put to work. It turned out to be a very good arrangement for all concerned. My grandfather was able to farm without worrying about the children, the children adored Helen the Holdeman girl, and Helen relished her so-called independence from her strict parents.

What happened next is predictable. My grandfather and Helen fell in love. How perfect for everyone, you might think, may they all live happily ever after, and may my grandmother rest in peace. Unfortunately, as usual, it was more complicated than that. When Helen's parents found out she was being courted by my grandfather they forbade her to remain in his employ, took her back home, and locked her in her upstairs bedroom. Why did they object so strongly to any type of romantic entanglement between their daughter and my grandfather? Not because he was an older widower in his early thirties with several dependent children, or that she was a minor, or that he was an impoverished farmer, or that he ate too many eggs, but because he was not a Holdeman, and Holdemans are forbidden to marry outside of their church. And of course at that time one did not have relationships outside of marriage. It would have been assumed that if my grandfather and the Holdeman girl were in love, that they were planning to marry.

So there was Grandfather, back to square one, except that now instead of losing one woman, he had lost two. The Mennonite church he belonged to grudgingly allowed its members to marry Holdemans, who would then become ordinary Mennonites, but Holdemans were not allowed to marry ordinary Mennonites, who were thought to be too liberal-minded, which is all relative considering that the Ordinary Mennonite Church used to shun and cast out members that bought soft-top cars, owned radios, danced, smoked, drank, doubted, or had red telephones installed in their homes or avocado-coloured fridges.

My grandfather managed to send a message to Helen. He would appear at her window the next day while her parents were at evangelistic meetings, and, if she were willing, they would go to the city together and elope! If not, he would understand (or try to) and never interfere with her again.

The next day at the appointed hour, my grandfather, perched on a ladder, appeared at her window (I suppose there were no dogs in the yard) and Helen gave him her answer: Yes! But accompanied by tears, no doubt, for she was only seventeen and about to leave childhood behind forever. One day she's locked up in her bedroom like an unruly child and the next she's the wife of a thirty-four-year-old farmer and stepmother of four! I wonder sometimes if, by eloping with Helen, my grandfather was acting selfishly, but that's a troublesome thought that brings into question the very nature of love and need and so on and I haven't the time to delve into it.

The two of them caught a train in Giroux and spent a day in the city of Winnipeg having their picture taken (not allowed by grandfather's church, too vain) and shopping for new clothes (ditto, clothes were to be made by hand) and, ultimately, being married by a justice of the peace (not done!).

I'm not sure who took care of the children while Helen and my grandfather were sinning in the city, but I imagine the older girl, who was to become my kindly Aunt Margaret, would have known how to prepare eggs at least.

For some reason or other, maybe because the elders of the church pitied my unfortunate grandfather, his wife's death, failing crops, hungry kids, or maybe because a collective inner secret part of them admired his pluck, who knows, they shunned him and his bride for three months only. My grandfather was required to confess his sins to the Brotherhood, a group of church elders, and then was asked to wait in the church lobby while the Brotherhood hammered out the details of his shunning. When the elders finally emerged from the sanctuary with the verdict, they found my grandfather slumped over on a wooden chair, fast asleep.

That is my favourite detail in the story. The Brotherhood could do with him what they liked. He had what he wanted. He and Helen went on to have thirteen children together in addition to Groutfodasch Abe and the three older kids at home.

10

I would like to have my grandfather here with me now, telling me even more about that time, perhaps dandling my father, Henry, on his knee. My father as a child, before the time he cried at Mrs. I.Q. Unger's kitchen table. It's interesting that my father, after a three-month depression spent in bed, became an egg producer! One would think he'd had enough of eggs. Or perhaps he realized their intrinsic value as they had kept not only him but his entire family alive in the years after his mother's death. Perhaps the egg came to symbolize comfort for my father. Perhaps the business of selling reasonably priced quality eggs was, in my father's mind, an act of kindness. It was my father's uncle, the brother of his mother, the woman who died of a blood clot at the age of twenty-six, who gave him a loan to start his egg business after denying him a raise at his job at the feedmill, after which sales at the feedmill plummeted.

As a young man, before I went to normal school (no jokes,

please), I worked for my father, delivering eggs to restaurants in the city. How I hated it! Some of these upscale restaurants had the filthiest kitchens I'd ever seen. I'd make mental notes of these deplorable conditions, going to elaborate lengths all my life to avoid having to dine at those establishments. Even as an older man, as a grandfather, I remembered the conditions of certain restaurants (bug infestation, vermin, rodents, mould, rot, mildew, animal droppings), some of which are still operating today.

I recall a time I made Elvira laugh. It's funny now because I hadn't thought it very funny then, if you know what I mean, but Elvira had been through some hard times and needed a bit of relief, I imagine. On this occasion she had accompanied me on my egg-delivery duties and our last stop of the day was the CN train station on Main Street. After dropping off the eggs I crumpled up the carbon copy of the receipt and dropped it down a stairwell in the station. I said, Call your floor, please! For some reason Elvira found my imitation of an Eaton's elevator lady hilarious, and it was some time before she could stop laughing and carry on any type of conversation. Of course, because I was me and not Benny Hill, I was more alarmed than flattered. I felt that her laughter was disproportionate to the strength of the joke, and I remember thinking I'd have to muzzle myself next time we were in public together to avoid the undue attention of strangers if she was going to laugh at the drop of a hat — or a carbon copy.

Later that same day, Elvira and I were enjoying Cokes in a local restaurant, and I guess I was talking a bit about my awful job, my hatred of chickens and eggs and so on, and in the course of this I must have mentioned the word "capons." Elvira, knowing very little about chicken farming, asked me what a capon was. I was flustered by the question. Er, well, a chicken that's . . . male, but . . . well, you know hens are females . . . er, and well, a rooster is . . . Elvira couldn't contain her laughter. I have often wondered if she had known all along what a capon was and was simply having another go at me.

∽

I have forgotten the time. I see red numbers on the clock radio but I don't know what they mean, or what they signify. It is the "time" I know, but . . . I have forgotten my call again, or have forgotten to make my call. How will I know when to do it? What is wrong with right now? Well . . . am I agitated? Check my file! And make a note: Dwindling spirits — Will rally. By the way, the impatient nurse has left my room. Her parting words: You're not helping yourself.

What I need to do at this time is follow Samuel de Champlain's example and establish an Order of Good Cheer. Unfortunately, the only other patient I know is Hercules, and he weighs less than four pounds and is going home soon anyway.

∽

In winter it was so cold that the apple cider froze in the barrels. At night the cold wind blew through the cracks of the crude log huts, while settlers, sick with scurvy, tossed and groaned in their rough beds. Each day brought more monotonous foods, more sickness and despair.

If I were to attempt to establish an Order here at the hospital, who would join? Apparently my days of establishing Orders of Good Cheer are as over, as are Champlain's. I always enjoyed that point in our studies. It was a favourite assignment of mine, a chance for my students to come up with extravagant costumes and often hilarious renditions of life in the early 1600s.

Put on a celebration of the Order of Good Cheer for the class. Dress in appropriate costumes, and perform songs and skits. Prepare some food the colonists at Port Royal might have eaten.

Every year the creativity and innovation of my students amazed me. I remember the year Jerry Goosen played the role of Champlain with such fiery intensity that he forced his scurvy-ridden settlers, at gunpoint, to "kneel" and "obey" and "now celebrate properly." Naturally a few of the girls began to giggle and one or two boys, pretending to be drunk on apple cider, made vomiting sounds, which so infuriated our young Champlain that he fired off a round of caps from the gun that he had earlier assured me was empty, while screaming at top volume for the real fun to begin. Obviously he had taken the Order of Good Cheer literally. I quickly intervened and told poor Jerry that a very loose adaptation of events was all that was needed and certainly gunfire was unnecessary. But Jerry then reminded me that Champlain had had a tendency to fire off his rifle at strange times, particularly while battling with the Iroquois. Yes, Jerry, I said, but this is the Order of Good Cheer. These are Champlain's own men! (And women: it wasn't historically accurate that women would have been involved with the Order, but we made this adjustment to accommodate the girls in the class who refused to dress up as men.) Yes, I know, said Jerry, but I have to be fierce with my own men because later they come up with a plot to murder me, which I barely escape. It says so in the book. And why would they want to kill a man they liked?

And it was true. Unfortunately, my principal at the time reprimanded me for flagrant misuse of the classroom and questioned my motives in allowing my students to dress up and "play act with loaded guns." Naturally I assured him that it wouldn't happen again and that the students had learned a lot from the exercise. But I was upset by his reaction.

Tell him to blow it out his ear, Elvira said as she slid a bowl of vanilla ice cream topped with the usual chocolate syrup, banana slices, and chopped walnuts across the kitchen table. Eat this, you'll feel better. Elvira and I, and later the girls, enjoyed this special dessert twice a day, after lunch and supper, for many, many years, and after the first bowl Elvira would always say, How 'bout another one? She could, when it came to ice cream, eat us all under the table. Some days I would come home from work to find her and her brother-in-law, Lorne (a diabetic!), hunkered over a tub of Heavenly Hash, spoons in hand, not even bothering with bowls, and competing for the soft, smooth ice cream that lined the outer edges of the cardboard container. Even in her early forties, when she announced that she was going on a diet consisting of half grapefruits and dry whole wheat toast, and beginning an exercise regimen that involved riding her blue bicycle twice around the town perimeter, she refused to give up her ice cream desserts. She insisted that, with the addition of the banana slices and chopped walnuts, they provided her with a complete protein.

Elvira, I believe, was the exclusive member of her own Order of Good Cheer, and from time to time I would tentatively enter its domain. A certain freedom of spirit accompanied her through life, and with it, I believe, a sense of security in the world. I don't know if she was born with it or if she acquired it over the years. Her home was generally a happy and prosperous one, and her parents loved her very much. She has told me many times that she felt that love consistently and that she carried it with her like a talisman through life. But there was sadness too, of course. Of the thirteen children (she was the thirteenth) born to her parents, six died before the age of two years and were buried all in a row with small stone markers in a cemetery not far from her home. Her mother, a quiet and pious woman, had not been her father's first choice, apparently,

and had been stood up by him a few times before they eventually married, only because the woman he had really wanted
to marry was forbidden by her brothers to have anything to do
with him. He'd been a bit of a rascal in his youth, though a
charming, irresistible one with a huge appetite for life and
a generosity of spirit that became legendary in the town.
Elvira's mother, who had been pregnant for most of her married life, died of high blood pressure when Elvira was fifteen
years old. Elvira finished her grade twelve in Winnipeg, at a
private Mennonite Bible college, where she was known as
a rebel: funny, wild, and independent. Her school yearbook
describes her as "a girl who drinks life to the lees!" She told me
it was the loneliest year of her life. She was so unhappy that
she intentionally avoided crossing bridges so she wouldn't be
tempted to throw herself into the river and drown. Afterwards,
her older brothers encouraged her to attend Bible school for a
year in Omaha (birthplace of Marlon Brando, incidentally).

11

MR. *TOEWS! IT IS IMPERATIVE* THAT YOU STOP
WRITING NOW! The nurse is angry. Why? Am I littering? Am I
clamouring for attention? YOU'RE ACTING LIKE A CHILD!
Well, it wasn't my idea to glue Popsicle sticks to a doily, was it?

∽∾

As a child I felt it was my responsibility to be someone who
would not bring more pain to my parents. I thought I had the
ability to control my father's quiet sadness and my mother's
drinking by bringing no extra hardship whatsoever to their
lives. That school photograph of our kindergarten class was
taken when I was five years old, shortly after my brother was
born. I have said that my hair was slicked into place with that
most universal of well-meaning gestures, a dab of my mother's
spit. It's not true. My mother, that morning of the school photo,
was sleeping late after a long night of drinking and crying, and

my father, overwhelmed as usual, had left early for work. Before leaving he had left a bun with honey on a plate for me, and had laid out my favourite beige sweater with the horizontal stripes, the one seen in the photo, on the table beside the bun. I vaguely remember standing in front of the mirror and staring at myself for what seemed like hours, trying to muster up the courage to spit on my finger and rub it on my head.

I don't recall having succeeded, but in the photo my hair is definitely slicked over to the side, and I imagine my teacher would have done it herself. I wonder what Elvira was doing that morning to prepare for the class photo. Chin-ups likely, considering how she seems to have muscled her way to the forefront of the shot.

I don't remember my parents being especially happy, or if they were, for a fleeting moment here or there, I felt in my heart that it wouldn't last, that it was unreliable, and I would become suspicious, wondering why it was there in the first place. My parent's brief bouts of happiness always had a ring of doom to them, at least to me, and whenever they occurred, instead of revelling in them I would brace myself for the inevitable aftermath of gloom.

I have had feelings of deep joy in my life, feelings of contentment, and pride, but only twice, perhaps, in my life have I felt free. That is, free to enjoy the moment with nothing in my mind other than the feeling of being free.

The first time it happened, as I have mentioned earlier, was when, while experiencing the effects of ether, I imagined myself to be somersaulting through the hospital walls. But because it was a drug-induced feeling, I tend to discount its validity. Therefore my one and only taste of absolute freedom, as I recall, occurred while skating with Elvira at the old school in Bristol, six miles southwest of Steinbach. This was the site of my first teaching job, after graduating from normal school. The Bristol school had two rooms, four grades in each. I taught the lower grades, from one to four. In the winter, I built a skating rink in the field next to the school, where my students and I spent many happy hours at play. While I was teaching in Bristol, I lived at home with my parents in Steinbach, and Elvira lived in Winnipeg, in the residence at Grace Hospital, where she was studying to become a nurse.

She and I were supposedly dating at this time, although, at least for me, the quality of our dates left much to be desired. Our "dates" consisted of attending the Wednesday-evening service together at the new Mennonite church on Beverley Street, in the city's west end. Afterwards, I would walk her home to her dorm and then drive all the way to Steinbach in my father's car, thinking of the clever things I should have said but didn't. I was only nineteen years old and I longed for more contact with Elvira, but nurses' training in those days was a gruelling, rigid program that allowed very little free time. Dating, especially, was discouraged because hospitals were not interested in training women to become nurses if, in the process, they were going to fall in love and get married. In those days, most married women did not work outside the home. Elvira has told me that while she was in training, she and all the other young women had to report to their dorm mother when they required sanitary napkins. This way the natural cycle of each woman could be tracked and, during fertile days, their chores at the residence could be doubled in an effort to prevent them from leaving the hospital grounds on dates. Of course, if a woman required no sanitary napkins for any length of time, it was assumed that she was pregnant and she was immediately expelled from the program.

Occasionally, if she was very lucky, Elvira was allowed to leave the premises for a longer period than was required to attend a church service. On one of these occasions it was arranged that I would pick her up in the car that I had bought for my parents (but had to ask for permission to use) and bring her out to Bristol, where we would spend the evening skating together.

It was a night in February, I believe, and mild enough that she and I could hold hands without wearing gloves. There we were in the middle of nowhere, really, alone in a field, in the dark, gliding around and around and around, nineteen years old and so in love with each other. We could see the outline of the little school and the moon and the ice beneath us and each other and that was all. Our lives, in that moment, were perfect. I was a teacher, she would soon be a nurse, we would get married in the church we had attended all our lives, build a home, and have children.

But it was more than this and perhaps the opposite of it that contributed to my feeling of being free. I don't know what it was exactly, if it was that I knew I would be leaving my parents' home soon, or that I felt in that moment finally at home in the world, or if it was because I was in between lives in a way, not a child under my parents' control, not too much anyway, and not yet a father and husband but just somehow existing outside of everybody's expectations. I sometimes wonder if at that moment somebody had come and tapped me on the shoulder and asked if I would be interested in walking away then, just walking off into the darkness alone, away from life as I knew it, with no plan whatsoever, what I would have said.

There was something about that feeling of absolute freedom that scared me and yet made me feel more alive than I'd ever felt before. I wonder if, later on in life, my rigid adherence to rules and conventional standards was a means of protecting myself from myself, from making sure I didn't follow that little voice and walk away. Not because I didn't love Elvira but because I also loved that feeling I had experienced on the ice.

Is it a self-destructive urge, I wonder, to want to walk away from everything you know and love, or not? Is depression in part a result of not feeling at home in this world, and blaming yourself for it? Is it similar to a battered woman's belief that she is the cause of her own misery, that somehow she brought the abuse upon herself, and if only she were a better wife, it might stop? Does a depressed person say to himself, if only I were a better human being I wouldn't feel depressed, or does he say, if only the world were a nicer place I might get out of bed?

Is depression nothing but anger turned inwards, as some say? Does it stem from a childhood loss? From a genetic propensity? From self-hatred? From an inability to be oneself? From having no purpose? From an inability to be free? From a fear of freedom? From the desire to be free and confined at the same time? From choking on a peanut as a two-year-old?

Perhaps depression is caused by asking oneself too many unanswerable questions.

❧

I recall an article I read yesterday in the *Free Press* re a young man's interview with the police. He had left his room and stabbed a fellow in the parking lot of his apartment block. I don't know why I did it, he told the cops. My head was so full of thoughts I couldn't make sense of anything. The only thing I felt was lonely. One minute I was lying in my bed trying to imagine the feeling of being loved by wrapping my own arms around myself, like this, and the next I've stabbed a man. I think I think too much, he said.

❧

I had never planned for this to happen. I want to scream but I fear I'd only end up scaring myself further.

12

I dread my brother's visits. I am supposed to talk to him about myself. I'm afraid I'll say something that will get me in trouble. This is a hospital, not a hotel, and E. is in the city resting. They say. Write. This is my brother's hospital. The girls say I'll be out very soon.

❧

Normally I encourage my students to go over their work with a fine-toothed comb several times before submitting it to me, but today I'll not follow my own advice. I remember asking Elvira to readdress, legibly, the invitations to our wedding after she had scrawled out a dozen or so, eventually ending up doing it myself. One time, much to her annoyance, I insisted that she erase the drawing she had made, in a letter to her sister in California, of the floor plan of our new house and replace it with a more accurate representation of angles and square footage, where one inch equalled ten feet and so on. Had I that capacity for precision of thought today, well, I suppose I might not be writing this, if writing is the result of a need to make sense of things.

But now I can't bring myself to read the slurred thoughts that managed to escape from my head and lurch across this page, and I don't have an eraser or whiteout, or the time to redo it, so I'll simply carry on. I was on the topic of freedom, as I recall, and if I wasn't, well, then I am now. Goodness, this room is getting warm. Perhaps I'll loosen my tie.

I have said that Elvira, while in her forties, went on a grape-fruit and toast diet and began to exercise. But that's not all she did while in her forties. One day she got out of bed and went into the bathroom. She looked at herself in the mirror and said, What will I choose? Freedom or insanity?

Those were her exact words. I know because she told me so herself years later. She may have told others too. For all I know it became a rallying cry for housewives all over town. Freedom or insanity! What can she have meant by freedom and what can she have meant by insanity?

But let me retrace my steps. By pretending to wonder what she meant I'm being coy. At the time, perhaps, I wondered. But today I know. There were things I expected of Elvira. I expected her to stay at home and be a housewife, to raise the children, to cook and clean, to accompany me to staff dos, to be somewhat involved in church activities, such as teaching Sunday school or attending Sewing Circle, to take care of my needs, and to be happy. More than anything, I needed her to be happy. I loved her, of course, and I truly believed that my expectations of her were fair and decent. She functioned and put on a brave front most of the time, but she wasn't herself. I had squelched her spirit, which was the very thing I loved about her. She was becoming sad. There is no joy involved in following others' expectations of yourself.

Elvira looked at herself in the bathroom mirror and chose freedom. She resumed her nursing career with a part-time job in the Steinbach Hospital Emergency Room (just down the hall; I bled there) and supplemented that income by working nearly full time as a receptionist for the local chiropractor. She arranged for a cleaning lady to clean our house once a week, she taught the girls how to operate the washing machine and dryer, she stocked the freezer with TV dinners and huge vats of ice cream, she attended social work classes at the University of Manitoba (from which I had recently graduated with my Master of Education), and with her earnings from her two jobs she booked a summer trip for all of us to South America (where we almost fell off a cliff into the Amazon River) and just hoped and trusted that those of us who loved her would continue to, and if not . . . she'd take that risk.

When I think back to those days now I can't believe how naive I was. I really thought that she had stopped loving *me*. I'd take the girls out for supper and put on a brave front, smiling and talkative, but I'd be thinking about Elvira and who she was meeting in these classes and would all this determination to be free result in her leaving me altogether. I was literally sick with anxiety. I didn't think about the fact that I had taken courses at the university too, very recently, and had enjoyed them, or of the satisfaction that working gave me, or of my own distaste for household chores and cooking.

Eventually I realized that Elvira wasn't leaving me and that she was much happier, and more affectionate, than before, and that the world hadn't come to an end. Only a few years later, when she graduated with her Bachelor of Social Work, I was the proudest husband in the land. Later, at Rae and Jerry's Steak House, the girls and I toasted to her success and she responded by thanking me for allowing her the freedom to go to school. But on the drive home I mulled over her comment and concluded that in fact I hadn't allowed her to do anything,

I had simply stood by and watched her do it, and that I wasn't worthy of her gratitude, and that furthermore, she had managed to do what she had done in spite of me and not because of me. That night while we lay in bed waiting to fall asleep I wanted to tell her that I was sorry, that she had only herself to thank, and that I would try to be more sensitive to her needs in the future. I wanted to tell her how proud I was of her and that I had been wrong in my previous evaluation of her role as my wife. I wanted to hold her and tell her how much I loved her and how grateful I was that she hadn't left me.

I may as well have wanted to stop time or bicycle to the moon. I remember the pain in my jaw where the words had stopped and the pressure of tears pushing against the inside of my forehead and some deep, deep force from within me making sure that not one teardrop fell and that not one word was uttered. I was prisoner and warden simultaneously, longing to free myself with words while going to every effort to prevent the words from escaping the darkness of my mind.

∽

Heard voices outside my door. Recognized them as belonging to sister and company. Feigned sleep, heard door open and close. Coast clear. Am wondering if people take literally the visiting hours sign. More work sure to be accomplished were sign changed to Visiting Minutes: 2-4.

13

As I recall, I was talking about eggs when the subject of freedom popped into my head and scrambled my senses. I have a low opinion of eggs. I have always associated them with weakness and pain. Their smooth white shell belies the sickly yellow, often blood-streaked, once-living trickle that slops around inside, buffeted by a slimy coat of clotted, milky gauze, and served with toast and bacon.

Sometimes, to counter the tedium of delivering those vile eggs, I would entertain myself with bizarre thoughts. For instance, one day I compared myself to an egg and was disturbed by the similarities. I thought of my own reasonably pleasant exterior and the yolk for brains that splashed around inside me. This yolk, it seemed to me, would always remain the same. As long as I worked as an egg-delivery "boy" my yolk would never grow into a living thing and hatch! I would remain unformed forever, while smiling nicely to the world and trying not to crack before my time. But my time would never come, because, according to my reasoning at the time, or lack thereof, I had been taken from the nest too soon. How to self-incubate the embryonic rooster in my head and flap my wings and fly away! I'm as crazy as an egg, I thought. Who will keep me warm before I break?

I remember driving back and forth over the Norwood Bridge in my father's truck saying to myself, I'm seventeen, I'm seventeen, because this was the only certain thing I knew about myself and I didn't want to forget it. Somehow the idea of having existed for seventeen years comforted me, and soon I was calculating the number of months and then weeks and then days and trying to tell myself that the numbers were good, that they implied a lot of living, that I had managed to do it. This gave me the confidence to get off the bridge and head for home.

When I got there I went directly to my bed and lay down, muttering, I mustn't break, I mustn't break, and Careful with my head, careful with my head, until my mother came into my room and told me to be quiet because Reg was studying for a test in the next room and wasn't to be disturbed. I wanted to speak to my father about quitting my job delivering eggs, but he wasn't at home and besides I knew that I needed the money for tuition, although at that point I didn't know exactly what I would be studying. Elvira was away at Bible school at this time, and I keenly missed her. I remember leaning over the edge of my bed to retrieve the last letter she'd written to me and thinking, Careful, don't drop it, but I was referring to my head, not the letter. I lay back and began to cry, finally, and I thought, It's over now, it's pouring out of me, my shell has cracked and I will never have another chance.

That was the last thing I remember of myself as an egg. The next morning or four days later, nobody told me how long it had been, I woke up here in this hospital and was diagnosed as suffering from manic depression. Hmm, I said when the doctor told me. Are you hungry? he asked. Hmm, I replied again. I was busy thinking. He left the room and I sat up and looked out the window. I told myself that soon I'd go home and things would be back to normal. I would become a teacher and I would marry Elvira and my life would have some purpose. And that was when I began to think of assignments that would help bring history to life for my students. (Write a lively account of one man's nervous breakdown!) I realized that by going over my life there on the bridge, all seventeen years of it, month by month, year by year, I was piling up the details in my mind, creating a type of solid base to stand on, and this somehow made my existence relevant to me, as though it had more weight than I had thought and more reason for being, that in fact it had come from something and not just materialized out of the blue.

A few minutes later a nurse brought me some breakfast and said, I hope you like eggs!

Several days later my doctor, whose name sounded something like Ratatatat, rocketed into my hospital room — he was always in a frightful hurry — and said, Melvin, it's time you went home, and so I did, leaving behind the various cards and tracts from Matthew, Mark, Luke, John, and Corinthians that the nurses had left for me to read. As I walked home I began to see things in a different light, or rather a sort of gothic half-light. Thankfully I had stopped comparing myself to an egg, but my mind was still far from settled, though of course it may have been the medication they had put me on while in the hospital, medication I would take for the rest of my life. But things were not as they had been. Everything around me, cars, houses, clouds, trees, dogs, people, seemed to have grown while I was in the hospital. Everything but the sun, which seemed to have shrunk to the size of a pea. I walked towards my house very slowly, wondering what I would say when I got there and what would be said to me.

About a block from my house I stopped and sat on the grass beside the road and closed my eyes. My head seemed to grow as quickly and roundly as though it were a balloon being inflated, and I put my hands up to feel it. My head, of course, was the same size it had ever been, but, with my eyes tightly shut and my hands tentatively patting the air two feet out from where my head really was, and what with all the medicine coursing through my veins, I toppled over.

Moments later I opened my eyes and was surprised to see a familiar face looming over me. It was Reg, sent by my mother to meet me along the way, to make sure, though this wasn't mentioned, that I didn't walk away from the town altogether or begin to run up and down its streets as I was accustomed to doing.

Hello! I said, genuinely relieved to see the little guy. Get up and come home, he said, you're in trouble.

Trouble! I thought. What have I done? As I stumbled home past overgrown houses and giant swaying sheds and trees the size of smoke stacks, I racked my head for clues. Had I lost a receipt book or dented my father's truck? Had I, in my earlier state, said something nasty to one of my father's major egg customers? Had I, during my stay in the hospital, introduced my parents to the doctors and nurses as Mr. and Mrs. Dumpty?

I found my family solemnly gathered around the kitchen table staring mournfully at a pink beef roast as though it were a recently deceased relative. My father looked up at me and pointed with his chin to an empty chair beside my sister. I took my place and, not knowing what else to do, began to stare also at the chunk of meat in the centre of the table. Finally, after a silent prayer, we began to eat. The only time my father prayed aloud was on the day before he died.

Nothing much was said during the meal, and I assumed that my brother had only been trying to frighten me with his comment. Later, however, my father asked me to come into the little room where he balanced his books. So . . . , he said in Low German, when you were at the hospital you mentioned to your doctor that Mother . . . His voice trailed off.

I didn't know what he was referring to, so I cocked my head and waited for him to finish. He removed his glasses and placed them carefully on his desk. Then, with both hands, he began to rub his brow and temples and cheeks, and almost every other part of his face and neck. I noticed how tired he was, how tired he had always been.

That Mother . . . , I reminded him gently. But just as I said the words, it struck me. Of course, I thought, this was about her drinking. The doctor, who was really a psychiatrist from Winnipeg, and who may not have been aware of the implications of a small-town confession, had asked me if there was anything bothering me, anything untoward happening at home, anything that might be making me feel sad. At first I had simply said no, nothing. But he persisted, and finally, more out of a desperate need for him to stop questioning me than anything, I blurted out these words: Mother drinks. And then, because he had seemed so happy with my response, and because I hadn't thought of any repercussions, as Father would later put it, I told the doctor that Mother wasn't kind when she drank, and that mostly she wasn't kind to me, and that I didn't know why it had to be me, only that it always was and I had stopped hoping that it would ever change.

I looked at my father. My face was on fire and my hands were numb. I had shamed the family, I had jeopardized our status in the community, and my father's livelihood. I had ruined my mother's reputation and undermined my father's efforts to cope by turning away from it.

I'm sorry, I whispered to my father.

❧

That night I had the first dream of a series that would run all my life. I dreamt that our home was no longer our home and that we had to live elsewhere. These new homes varied in my dreams; sometimes they were bamboo houses on stilts, sometimes apartments in the city, sometimes underground parking lots. Once, it was a foul-smelling greenhouse with hanging ferns and piles of moist earth everywhere. Each time we moved, we ended up wanting to go back, but for whatever reason — the house had been sold, or we couldn't afford moving costs — it was impossible to do so.

Sometimes Elvira, sensing that I'd had one of my dreams, would ask me in the morning: So? Where were we living last night?

Over the years, my dream expanded to include the "homelessness" of friends and casual acquaintances. Eventually nobody I knew was allowed to live in their homes. Everybody was living elsewhere, usually unhappily but not always, and wanting to return to their original homes.

I realize that this dream is quite obvious in its meaning: I'm looking for a home, or for a sense of home, or for my self, but I can't find it. I rather doubt its uniqueness.

What is interesting about my dream, is that it has come true. It has stopped being a dream with metaphorical significance and has become reality, as though the dream all those years had been an exercise in preparation for the real event. Perhaps God is trying to give me a sign. Or perhaps it was simply a premonition.

❧

Everything's in boxes. We're moving to the city, apparently. I'm a little worried about it. Girls say it'll be fine, hard at first, but okay later. Somebody's looking after the yard. That's good. They say: Mom's in the city, she's moving there. It's the only way they'll transfer you to a place where you'll get the right care. If she goes home, they'll find out and send you back there. She can't take care of you on her own anymore, but nobody believes her.

That's your fault for saying you are fine, they don't say. They say nothing is my fault, and I wish they wouldn't say that. How can a man be forgiven if nothing is his fault? I'm sorry for the death of E. And the pilot. I keep saying it, but nobody will listen.

❧

That evening, the evening I was discharged from the hospital, after my chat with Father and before the dream, I hung around a bit outside listening to the wind and the chickens, chewing on my thumbs and wondering what was to become of me. I sat on the back steps and penned a letter to Elvira.

Dear Elvira, I began. By now you've probably heard, from your brothers or from Roy or Martha, that I spent some time recently thinking I was an egg, and as a natural result of that, was hospitalized for incubation, I mean, observation. The upshot of it all is that I'm myself again, for what that's worth, and I've decided I want to become a teacher. First an egg, now a teacher! I wish I had more of your ability to remain the same over a period of time. Of course I'll have to begin my training soon, which would, I'm quite sure, necessitate a move to the city. How's Uncle Sam? How are you enjoying your studies? Are you able to socialize as much as you like to? Things here are exactly the same, except of course for my egg episode and that a new expansion is being added to the church. I think teaching will be right for me. I hope so anyway. Are you frightened by me now, or will our relationship remain secure? I feel quite all right now, and I imagine the worst is over.
As Ever, M.

I didn't know how to work in the fact that I had, by opening my mouth and uttering two words, ruined the lives of my parents and brother and sister, and so I just left the letter as it was and the next morning I mailed it to Omaha. My father had given me a few days off of work to rest up, and I didn't want to spend all day at home with Mother.

I decided that I would build something out back behind the feed shed and try to think of ways to improve relations with my family. I should have wondered at that time about my father's own bout of despair and about his three-month stay in bed after leaving the feedmill. But it didn't occur to me then, or ever, to ask him. If only I'd kept my mouth shut, I repeated to myself as I hauled my tools and wood to the shed.

Who knows why, maybe it was the precariousness of my mind at that time, or because I was so determined to come up with a new life strategy, becoming a teacher, a better person, et cetera, or because I was young, or because I didn't want to lose Elvira, or because I didn't want to be crazy, or because I still wanted somehow to fit into my family, or because I still felt there was a slim chance I'd impress my parents with my industriousness and that this might erase the hurt I had caused them by talking to the doctor, but I came up with an altogether bad plan for the future: To keep my mouth shut. If, in the months and years to follow, I had only taken stock of the situation I would have realized that no undue hardship had fallen on my family. My father didn't lose his egg business, and my mother's reputation in the church and community hadn't changed one bit. We weren't excommunicated. My brother wasn't tarred and feathered by local bullies or taken away by child welfare authorities. Nothing had changed. If I had known then what I know now, I would have known that there was no stronger power in this town than the power of denial.

But it seemed so simple and right at the time. I remember leaning against the wall of the feed shed and thinking that, because the sun had moved over to shine directly on me as I made my decision, God had somehow sanctified it, and that the brilliance of the sun was equal to the brilliance of my plan. I decided that I would get busy with my hands and get my mind off myself by making a pair of stilts for my friend and neighbour D.W. Later in the day I would teach him how to walk and then run on the stilts, and the two of us could race each other down Town Line Road!

I worked on the stilts all day, modelling them after my own set, which Father had made for me years before, and in the evening when D.W. came home from school, I told him what I had planned. It won't take you long to learn, I said, we could be racing later tonight! I had, in my earlier childhood, spent many enjoyable hours running through town on my stilts but, as I told D.W., I'd never had anybody to race with. Surprisingly, he agreed. After supper, he and I went out to the feed shed to retrieve the stilts. We practised in the field as the sun fell below the horizon and the sky turned purple. I suppose I should have taken the sun's disappearance as a sign that the brilliance of my plan was also fading. D.W. could walk well enough on the stilts but he couldn't quite get the hang of running and kept lifting his foot off the block in midstride and falling into the dirt. It's not like normal running, D.W., I'd tell him, your legs shouldn't bend at the knees. Think of your legs as straight pieces of wood, as one with the stilts.

But no amount of counselling could rid D.W. of his habit of running "on top" of the stilts, and I could tell he was becoming discouraged. I was about to suggest to him that we try again the next day when, suddenly, I had another idea. The sun, at that very moment, likely dropped entirely out of view if I am to think that its brightness coincided with the brightness of this idea. I would tie his legs to the stilts!

Sure enough, in a matter of moments, with the help of a roll of twine found in the feed shed, D.W. had managed to stay

with his stilts. Soon he was running, with only moderate awk-
wardness, through the dirt, and I knew the time had come. I
didn't want to go to the trouble of untying D.W. from his stilts,
so I brought the truck around and dragged him into the back of
it, stilts and all, and hopped into the cab. In a matter of minutes we were at Town Line Road, ready to race. By now it was
pitch black outside, and except for the sound of crickets in the
ditches, deathly quiet. We could smell the fresh spring clover
and the dust from the road. I had already made up my mind
that I would win by only a very narrow margin, so that D.W.
might feel motivated to race me again with the hope of win-
ning. I asked him if he was having fun, and he said he was. Are
you nervous? I asked him, and he said of course he wasn't. If I
could do it, he could do it. Fair enough, I said, then let's do it!

We had agreed to run from the truck to the beginning of
W.F. Harder's green fence, which was about a quarter of a mile
down the gravel road. We left the truck headlights on so we'd
be able to see where we were going. We stood on each side of
the cab, using it to steady ourselves before we began. On your
mark, I said, get ready . . . I glanced at D.W. . . . go!

And there we were, flying along Town Line Road in the dark
like a couple of giant stick insects. Right off the top I pulled
ahead of my friend, just to set the pace and get him going, but
after half a minute or so I pulled back and let him take the
lead. The heel of his stilt must have caught a small stone as he
passed me and it flew up and hit me in the neck. By now most
of the light from the highbeams had been swallowed by the
dust we'd kicked up, and I slowed down even more, hoping
that D.W. would notice and take it easy. I didn't want him to
lose his way in the darkness and stumble into the ditch. He
must have noticed that I'd fallen back, because I could hear
him laughing, and that's when the accident occurred.

W.F. (Mennonite men of a certain age are almost exclusively
referred to by their first initials), we found out later, had been

awakened by his dogs, who were barking up a storm because of the ruckus D.W. and I were causing, and had, in a foul temper, jumped into his truck to investigate. He peeled out of his driveway and, not knowing we were there, drove straight at us. With all the dust in the air and D.W.'s loud laughter drowning out the sound of W.F.'s truck, it wasn't until it was immediately in front of us that we noticed it. Jump! I screamed at my friend, meaning off his stilts and into the ditch, but of course that was impossible because I had tied his legs to his stilts with twine. Because he was running, and because he was on stilts, it was impossible for him to change direction quickly and head for the ditch. He tried, of course, but the front bumper of W.F.'s truck clipped the end of one of his stilts. He sailed over the ditch and landed up against the green fence (he won!) on the other side.

I had easily abandoned my own stilts, of course, and was standing by the side of the road screaming for W.F. Harder to stop. I remember thinking that now, after hitting my friend, he would carry on in his rage and have a head-on collision with my father's truck, which was still parked and idling in the middle of the road. Again, I was wrong. W.F., by swerving to the right and flipping his own truck over onto its back, and breaking his collarbone, managed, heroically, to avoid crashing into my father's truck.

W.F. Harder was hospitalized in the city and D.W. was spending the night here in this hospital, after being X-rayed for broken bones. Mother reminded me of my vast array of short-comings and Father went into his room and closed the door.

That night, I read and reread all of Elvira's letters to me, each one signed with our traditional "As Ever" and I thought, I have nothing, nothing at all but her.

14

I couldn't wait for Elvira to finish her year in Omaha. She only had two months to go, but it seemed to me like a lifetime. Three days before she was due to arrive back in town, her brother George stopped me on the street and asked me if I'd come to a welcome home party he and her other brothers and their wives were throwing for her. He said it was a family party but I'd probably be part of the family soon so I could come too. Then he put his arm around my shoulder and winked at me!

I had no idea that she had ever mentioned me to him, let alone implied that we were planning to be married. I hadn't even found the courage to kiss her yet. If I hadn't stopped taking signs from the sun I would have thought the intense warmth of that day's sunshine was a harbinger of good things to come. I was very fond of Elvira's older brothers, and to be accepted into this jovial family made me want to sing with joy.

At the party, held in her father's large home, we played ping-pong on the dining-room table, a pair of Elvira's old nylons strung across as a net, and supervised the nieces and nephews as they slid down the stairs on cookie trays. We fed the bear cub they kept in the backyard farmer sausage and vrenike, we watched in awe as George, Edward, and Cornie consumed vast amounts of pie, and we fetched blankets for Johnny, the simple man who slept in the back porch when he'd had too much to drink and couldn't make it home. Elvira told us hilarious stories of her American classmates and their opinions of Canada, and Elvira's father gave us three bars of Lowney's chocolate each.

As the evening progressed, the most extraordinary thing of all occurred. The story of my fiasco involving D.W. and W.F. Harder came up. Elvira's brothers could barely tell the story without crying tears of laughter. I was horrified that it had come up at all, because I had intended for Elvira never to have to hear it. I had hoped that we would move to the city, she in her nurses' residence and I in my teachers' residence, complete our training, move back to town, marry, have children, and never speak once of the incident. Now here were her brothers laughing hysterically as they attempted to relay each and every detail of that hideous experience!

I managed to chuckle along here and there, keeping a close eye on Elvira so as to gauge her reaction. Naturally she laughed as hard as they did, and then, when at last the story had been told, she squeezed my sweat-soaked hand, sighed, and said affectionately, Oh, Mel, ha die nich dum.

After the party she announced to her family that she would walk me home. Her brother George issued a brief warning: No stilt racing! We left the house amid gales of laughter and wandered into the darkness of the night. Elvira maintained a running monologue, skipping merrily from one subject to the next, while I battled internally with my plan to somehow, in a seemingly natural way, get ahold of one of her hands, which were flying and flapping and fluttering about like two crazed white doves trapped in a milk crate. I would soon learn that every member of her family spoke with their hands. There is a well-circulated story here in town of C.T., Elvira's father, who, one day, was deep in conversation with a friend of his. They were standing outside and it was very cold, and C.T. was doing all of the talking. Finally, he stuffed his bare hands into his pockets and told his friend, "Now it's your turn to talk, my hands are cold."

I wish I could tell you that the sky was full of stars and that the warm, clover-scented breeze ruffled our hair, or that my voice had a husky timbre to it and my complexion was clear and Elvira's laugh tinkled like a Japanese wind chime, and that everything from that magical day on fell into place. The truth is that I was so consumed with love and need and longing and confusion that I can't for the life of me remember the details of what happened. Except for one, and that one I'll never forget. As Elvira and I clumped along through P.J. Guenther's freshly tilled potato patch, her shoelace came undone, and we stopped for a minute so she could retie it. She was wearing flat black and white saddle shoes and thin white socks. As she bent to tie her shoe, I looked at my useless hands and willed myself to move them, to do something with them, anything other than dangle them at my sides like Muschel Heinz, who spent his entire life sitting in front of the post office with a grimy book of stamps in his lap, ready, with postage, for the day he was to be delivered unto the Lord.

I'm seventeen years old, I thought, my girlfriend's back in town after a year's absence, it's dark, we're alone in a potato patch, she still, miraculously, likes me, and I'm acting like a side of beef on a freezer hook. At that moment my hands began to move, rather convulsively and quite involuntarily, like a nearly drowned person who, after being resuscitated, begins to vomit, and I reached out and placed my right hand just below her shoulder as if to steady her. I kept my hand on her back as she rose to her full height of five feet and I smiled briefly, in a casual way I hoped wouldn't terrify her, stooped, and kissed her on the mouth.

After the kiss, which lasted for a good three seconds, I looked at Elvira like a schoolchild looks at his teacher after completing a math problem at the blackboard, and she smiled and said, Correct! No, she didn't. She smiled and said nothing. But she took my hand and held it all the way to my house.

I realize it's slightly unusual for a girl to walk a boy home, but if she hadn't done so we wouldn't have had the opportunity to kiss in P.J. Guenther's potato patch, and knowing her like I do I can't help but think she had it planned.

Years later, when she and I were both twenty-four or twenty-five, I happened to be flipping through Elvira's Bible. I was teaching a Sunday school class and I must have been looking for a certain verse in I Corinthians to use in my lesson. She had various verses that she found significant underlined, just as I had in my own Bible. In my search for this particular verse I hadn't bothered to read what she had underlined until I came to chapter 6 of I Corinthians, verse 18. With a very faint pencil, she had underlined the first two words of the verse: Flee fornication!

Many thoughts rushed through my head at that moment. This particular Bible of hers had been given to her by her parents on Christmas Eve in 1949, when she was fourteen years old. I knew for a fact that, since we'd been married, she had used a different, more modern edition of the Bible (which I loathed), and so, I surmised, she must have underlined "Flee fornication!" in pencil when she was a teenager, and, I further surmised, she would not have underlined these stern words as a reminder if she had not been tempted. Therefore, I concluded, she had had feelings for me that were similar to the feelings I'd had for her, which meant that I hadn't been such a gangly, undesirable no-account after all!

Later that evening, after putting Marjorie to bed, I showed Elvira the words she had underlined and of course she laughed like there was no tomorrow. I didn't even know what it meant! she howled. We were kids! Imagine! she cried, I'm running for the hills, fleeing fornication, and you're right behind me breathing down my neck! And little do I know as I'm running for my life, she elaborated, that you're fleeing it too and not even interested in my . . . temple! The tears spilled onto her cheeks. I must admit I found it funny too, but I'm not so sure she was telling the truth when she said she hadn't known what it meant. Her faith in a loving and forgiving God is strong, but she worships laughter.

Even today, I like to think, for my own amusement, that she had known and that she had underlined those words the very day of the party knowing she'd be alone with me later and understanding all too well the proclivities of her flesh, and that only God had stopped her from melting in my arms that evening and pulling me down, knees buckling, into the coarse earth of P.J. Guenther's potato patch.

$\mathcal{L}15$

A nurse has, again, asked me about my writing. I'm writing about a few things that have happened in my life, I told her. Something to do to pass the time. Do you know why, for instance, I enjoy teaching grade six most, of all the grades? No, she said, kindly not mentioning that I'm not teaching any grade at this moment, why? Because, I answered, at the grade six level, children can read, write, and reason. Well, she said, I guess that's pretty important. Very important, I corrected her, very important. Yeah, I guess, she said. Now wait a minute, I felt like saying, how can you guess? How can you guess that reading, writing, and reasoning are important? How is it that you do not know? How is it that you have become an adult, I wanted to ask her, without knowing the importance of being able to reason? But, she said, I'm kind of curious about something, Mel — how come you can remember parts of your life from back whenever but, like, you can't remember who your visitors are now, and, you know, when you talk to your wife, and stuff like that. I had no idea what to say. Because, she went on, that's sort of like reason, right? I mean, like, in terms of knowing what's going on right now? Yes, I suppose so, I said, thoroughly confused. It dawned on me that this nurse believed me incapable of rational thought, that I had slipped, mentally, below the average capacity of an eleven-year-old. This nurse regarded me as she would a child. I felt my face flush, and I mumbled something about old age re the ability to remember details of an event that occurred fifty years ago but not necessarily what you had for dinner the night before. Even as I said it I knew she wouldn't buy it. She patted my hand, though, and murmured, Mel, I know you're insane. No, no, she didn't. She said, Mel, I know you're in pain. Before she left she promised to bring me an extra dessert from the kitchen. How can I ever thank her enough? (I'm ashamed of my lack of gratitude. She is doing her best.)

What's Mr. Toews up to? One nurse to another in the hallway.
   Oh, about six-two, says the other.

⁓

As the weeks passed and W.F. (Whiplash) Harder's collarbone mended itself, my resolve to become a teacher grew. I continued to deliver eggs all through the spring and summer of '53, and in the fall I began my training in the city. There were two things, however, that were bothering me. First of all, Elvira had told me that she was interested in becoming an airline stewardess after completing her nurses' training. The idea of her flying around the world in airplanes frightened me, and I knew I couldn't bear to lose her in a crash or in some sort of crazed hijacking scheme. Not only that but she would be gone for days at a time, I thought, and I would miss her terribly.
   So I went out of my way to draw her attention to tragic

news items having to do with airplanes. More people die in cars, Mel, she said. Then I pointed out that she would be gone for two or three consecutive days at times, and she said, Isn't it wonderful? I kept my mouth shut and hoped that she would, during the three years of nurses' training, change her mind.

The other thing that was bothering me was that I hadn't told her I was on medication for manic depression and would be, in all likelihood, for the rest of my life. I realized that if we were to be married she would have to know about it, but I simply didn't have the nerve to tell her then. I suppose this marked the beginning of my "quiet" life, the first phase of my plan to remain silent when it came to matters of myself.

❧

Normal school. Do you remember that time of life in the autumn of one's adolescence when a thousand hopes and dreams seem to clash with the realities of the world? That's what I think of when I remember normal school. Before I started normal school, I had big plans for my future classroom. When I finished normal school I still had big plans, but I realized how difficult it would be to see them through. It seems, as I think about it, that every step along the way of my career I had to beg and fight and pay to teach the way I wanted to. I would begin lessons from the texts provided, but as my students expressed interest in various topics or issues, we would veer off the beaten track and create an entirely new and innovative course of study. In my classroom this type of activity was officially known as trailblazing, and it was, by far, the students' favourite time of the day. They would lead discussions and come up with questions they thought were relevant, we would write many letters to members of the federal and provincial governments asking them to tell us about their jobs and how they hoped to help Canadians, we would run mock elections, we would work together on group projects (my favourite teaching activity), we'd build replica trading posts and reading lofts with big cushions and publish a class newspaper to let the entire community know what we were up to. We'd be kind to each other. We'd build birdhouses in the spring. We'd write and produce plays and memorize poetry and play a lot of baseball in the month of June!

I would prepare my students for the world outside, beyond our little town, and I would teach them to express themselves. In this way I could stay put and remain silent, in self-defence. There's no secret here, not really. Any psychiatrist worth his or her salt could tell you: My students' accomplishments would be mine. They would take my dreams and make them real.

In normal school, the emphasis was on discipline, how to control a group of thirty or more students, and structure, how to teach a varied group of individuals with little or no deviation from the standard textbooks provided. Basically the focus was getting them in, keeping them in, and getting them out. There was no emphasis on the joy of learning or the flexibility required to teach young children or the art of bringing a textbook to life. There were no discussions having to do with self-expression, or world-readiness, or group projects, or the necessity of sometimes having to veer from the text or write one's own, which I eventually did, or of the social relevance of all-day baseball tournaments in the month of June. There was no fun quotient, as they say, in normal school, and I hated it.

My write-up, however, in the 1954 *Mirror*, the normal school yearbook, reads as follows: "Melvin is interested in Sunday school work . . . enjoys most sports . . . a conscientious fellow working hard to do his duty." I was very pleased with this assessment.

I've thought of something. I will write my way out of this mess! I will fool myself. If I can continue to remember right up to the present, then I will know why I'm here. Slowly, I will creep towards the present, step by step, memory by memory, and my mind will then be eased, gradually, into a place of understanding. It will be very natural. Am very excited with new strategy. Pens, paper, must have, and to begin, now.

❧

After graduating from normal school, I moved back home to Steinbach and began my teaching career at the little two-room school in Bristol. I was nineteen years old, six foot two, one hundred and forty pounds, terrified, and proud. Elvis Presley, also nineteen, was about to change the course of history, but Elvira and I had never heard of him, and wouldn't for years to come. Our lives consisted of church, school, nurses' training, and planning our future, which had nothing to do with rock and roll.

My parents, particularly my mother, were not entirely pleased with my choice of girlfriend. Elvira came from the wealthiest family in town, and one with a colourful reputation. They were the first family in town to own a piano, for example (frowned on by conservative Mennonites at the time), and Elvira's father, C.T., (his brothers were J.T., P.T., I.T., and A.T.; the T. stands for Toews, their mother's maiden name) encouraged his sons to sow their wild oats before settling down into the family lumber business, which would eventually turn them all into millionaires. Elvira and I are second cousins, a typical occurrence in Mennonite couples. Her dad's mother was a sister to my dad's father, and it's a common Mennonite practice to give a child his mother's maiden name as a middle name. My daughters' surnames, if we hadn't nipped that interesting practice in the bud, would have been Toews Loewen Loewen Toews.

Elvira accompanied her father on many business trips and

working lunches at fancy restaurants (places I had delivered eggs to) in the city, regularly coming into contact with important businessmen and generally enjoying a worldly outlook on life. Once, when she was fourteen years old, she and her father drove to B.C. for a holiday visit with relatives. C.T. let Elvira do the driving, even through the Rocky Mountains with their treacherous hairpin curves. She adored her father and he loved her very much and very well. That is, he encouraged her to be herself and told her nothing was impossible. He expected her to be brave and honest and adventurous like he was. The fact that he had buried six of his thirteen children seemed not to have crushed his spirit. I remember an occasion when a rival lumberman was angry with him for some reason and making nasty threats, and C.T. casually telling me on his front porch, "He can kill me but he can't scare me."

But my mother was not altogether pleased with my association with the Loewens, of whom I was becoming increasingly more fond as the months went by, especially of Elvira, of course. I think my mother's reason for not liking the Loewens had to do with money, although I'm not entirely sure. The Reimer clan, of which my mother was a member, had been the wealthiest family in town until the Loewens came along and raised the stakes. It's assumed by many that Mennonites care little of money and material goods, but the very opposite is true. Anyway, my grandparents' general store gradually went broke because of the youthful carousing of my mother's brother, who was supposed to be in charge, while C.T.'s business flourished to become the largest and most lucrative in all of southeastern Manitoba. C.T. was also establishing a reputation as a fair and compassionate employer who took the complaints and advice of his workers to heart.

My mother, rather than placing the blame on her brother's shoulders for the failure of their family business, begrudged the Loewens for the success of theirs.

But my mother was not the only one to disapprove of our relationship. Elvira's mother, had she been alive, would surely have found it troublesome that Elvira was planning to marry the son of the cousin of her husband's first love, the woman who, as I have mentioned, was forbidden by her brothers to marry Elvira's father because of his rogue tendencies and worldliness. Little did her brothers know that C.T. would go on to become a very wealthy and respected man both in and out of the church and, unfortunately, that their sister, C.T.'s first love, would suffer a terrible accident with some permanent damage and remain a spinster for life.

It seems odd that Helena, Elvira's mother, such a gentle, pious woman normally, would harbour such a resentment of the Reimer clan, and that my extremely tenuous connection to her rival would have made me an undesirable son-in-law, but we must remember that she had been stood up at the altar by C.T. the first time they tried to get married, all because of this Reimer girl. Elvira's oldest brother married a girl from the Reimer clan and she and her mother-in-law had, at best, a strained relationship. Why Helena didn't direct her wrath at her husband, the more deserving target if ever there was one, is anybody's guess. Although the traditionally submissive role of Mennonite wives may have had a lot to do with it.

Nevertheless, our love blossomed and we were very happy with each other. My home life was troublesome still, but I knew I'd soon be leaving it behind. As soon as Elvira had completed her nurses' training we would be married and on our own. On the day of our wedding, December 28, 1956, Elvira would receive her inheritance with which to build our home at 229 First Street, and a new bedroom suite as a gift. By then I would be teaching grade six at Elmdale School in Steinbach, a seven-minute walk from home down First Street, up William, and across Main, a journey I'd make at least twice a day for forty years.

clorⳇ⳿

A friendly male nurse has entered my room to tell me that I am
not what I said I was, that I am being too hard on myself.
Now, I cannot remember what I said I was. What did I say I
was? I asked him. You said, Mel es en schinde, and that is not
true. But of course it is, I say, schinde is a Low German expression meaning "lower than low," originally, I believe, one who
tortures horses, a taskmaster, a tyrant. I am personally responsible for Elvira's demise, I intone rather formally. I drove her to
despair. No, says the nurse, you did not. You are ill, that's not
your fault. How naive and kind of him, I think as he pats me
on the shoulder. I notice our watches are similar and point this
out to him. He is excessively pleased. He is the same chap
who informed me that there are unusually high numbers of
Mennonites who suffer from depression but nobody knows
why. I said, Well, thank you for that! As cheerfully as if I was
accepting a plate of homemade Christmas cookies from one of
my students.

clorⳇ⳿

During this time, I was fairly optimistic. I had met my goal of
becoming a schoolteacher and I was in love with a wonderful
girl. Two years later we were married, and I have mentioned
already the somewhat chaotic circumstances of our wedding
ceremony re the candelabra, the burning veil, Wilma's race to
fetch another.

Several months before the wedding I had gone to Elvira's
brothers with a proposition. I knew that a woman of her background could expect to receive, usually from her parents, a
wedding gift of fine silverware. But Elvira's mother had died
years before and her father in the meantime had become
bedridden after a stroke. With all of my expenses at home and

my meagre teacher's salary I couldn't even begin to dream of purchasing the silverware myself. I asked the brothers, who were generous but busy with their own lives, if the three of them could pay for fifty percent of the cost of the silverware; I would pay the other half. They agreed on the spot, and Elvira was thrilled and surprised when I told her how I had financed the gift, a beautiful red-velvet-lined mahogany box of sparkling silverware. She has taken excellent care of the silverware ever since, using it only on special occasions, avoiding the dishwasher and washing it by hand, and, before it became one of the cleaning lady's pet projects, polishing it to the point of nearly blinding our dinner guests.

✺

Have just received a visitor who tells me I'm looking good. Oh, I don't think so, I said. Secretly was very happy to be told that I look good. Daughters tell me I'm handsome every day in my new Tommy Hilfiger shirt. Wish I could remember his name, assume he's a church elder because of the nature of our one-sided conversation. Offered him my dessert. Declined. Hope it wasn't tube food. I sat in silence, nodding at various intervals and smiling. Hope I thanked him for the visit. Should consider investing in a guest book. Would have names written down, comments. Would give me a clue.

16

Sometime before we were married I found the courage to tell Elvira that I had been diagnosed as a manic depressive and that I would likely be on medication for the rest of my life. She told me that she already knew this because she had found my pills in my pocket and had recognized what they were. She told me that she loved me and that everything would be fine. This statement proved to be half right: she loved me very much, though to this day I wonder how. My psychiatrist had, when I informed him that I was planning to get married, expressed no small amount of shock and dismay. He told me that those who suffer from manic depression have a lot of difficulty making marriages or any long-term relationship work, and when I told him that I was also planning on becoming a schoolteacher, he almost hit the roof. The responsibility, Mel, the consistency, the patience, the endurance . . . all these things are extremely difficult to maintain with an illness like yours . . . won't you reconsider? But of course I wouldn't. If anything at all, it was those two things, my marriage and my career, that kept me tethered to the ground, that made my life bearable and kept me from becoming unhinged.

The other worry of mine in those days, the possibility that Elvira would become an airline stewardess, was doused the day we married. So too was the possibility of her continuing her job as a nurse in the local hospital. There was only one married woman working in the hospital at that time and only because her husband had been injured and couldn't work.

In those days, in the early fifties, I was making $170 a month. We paid fifty dollars a month to rent the small motel room, next to my aunt Molly's laundromat, that we lived in for a portion of the time that our house was being built. Another fifty dollars a month went towards the payment of our house lot, and thirty dollars was our average monthly grocery bill. That left us with forty extra dollars a month. Had times been different, Elvira would have kept her job, which paid more than mine, and we would have enjoyed a much higher standard of living, not to mention the sense of fulfillment she would have had working in her chosen career. But in that respect, we were no different than any other couple of that era.

Those early years were good, bearable. No lengthy, inexplicable silences, no blackouts. We had two gardens, one each for flowers and vegetables, numerous flowerbeds all over the yard that got bigger every spring as I tilled the grass to plant more rows of red and white petunias. We had chokecherry trees and saskatoonberry trees and crabapple trees and later two willow trees that I planted in honour of the births of our daughters. In the front of the house, running almost its entire length, was a brick planter full of red and white petunias, and at the foot of the narrow paving-stone path that led from our front door to the street stood a huge and ancient elm tree. When Marjorie was a little girl, she would stand under this elm and wait for me to come home for lunch. Right outside our bedroom window was a wonderful-smelling evergreen that grew to an enormous height and width. I have a photograph of Marjorie standing beside the tree. They are the same height and she is seven years old. Elvira and I would often stand on the front porch and watch the sun set behind its boughs. Our house was made of red brick and I had painted the wooden part of it a dusty rose, my favourite colour, though the girls maintained we lived in a pink house.

Later, because of the amount of time I spent in bed, I became good at identifying sounds, in particular the individual noises of each family member. Marjorie played the piano from sunup to sundown, and my youngest, Miriam, slammed the front door countless times a day as she ran in and out of the house with friends. And Elvira talked on the phone or in the yard to friends, neighbours, and anybody else that came along. I couldn't decipher exactly what she was saying from my bed but I could hear a quiet steady rumbling punctuated with whoops of laughter and screams of No! or Not really! And Oba yo! (Oh, but yes!) and Oba nay! (Oh, but no!) Elvira could spend hours on the telephone and Miriam would sometimes, to get her attention, tie Elvira to the kitchen chair with her pink skipping rope. Or she would write notes to her mother such as: "I'm having difficulty breathing. My vision is blurry. Please tell your friend you'll call her back after you've performed CPR on me."

In the evening, if Elvira and the girls were out or watching TV together in the den, I would wander around the house picking up scraps of paper that had writing on them. Silly notes written by my daughters, grocery lists, receipts, and odd things doodled on the edges of newspapers and flyers, phone messages to the girls, pages ripped out of school notebooks that had been used to work out answers to math questions and discarded. I put all these papers into my filing cabinet in a folder marked "Family."

Our friends and neighbours on the block included the Steingarts, the Shilstras, the Schellenbergs, and the Schroeders, as well as the Bergers, the Barkmans, the Bubberts, and the Broeskys.

Mrs. Steingart, a well-meaning widow, lived directly across the street and knew as much as she needed to know about every aspect of life on our block. Often she would come into our house — our doors were never locked — and wash the dishes and tidy up. She never quite understood, but always accepted, Elvira's intense hatred of housework, and she was always happy to pitch in.

Miss Shilstra was a hermit who lived in a haunted house, according to the children on the block. In truth, she was a kind, eccentric, independent woman, the unmarried daughter of two medical doctors, who lived alone in an ancient weather-beaten house amidst piles and piles of yellowing newspapers. At Christmas and Easter, Elvira would insist that one of the girls take Miss Shilstra a plate of baked goods that she'd prepared for the holiday. On these occasions Miss Shilstra would invite whoever had been given the task in for a cup of tea. The girls, I noticed, seemed oddly exhilarated each time they'd had a visit with old Miss Shilstra, perhaps because they felt they had narrowly survived the situation.

Between Miss Shilstra and Mrs. Steingart lived the Schroeders, a friendly family and home to the ever-adventurous Debbie, Miriam's best friend throughout elementary school. As a child Debbie stayed up until one every morning to watch Merv Griffin on TV and every morning was raring to go before any other kid on the block. Every day, after school, she headed off to the Five to a Dollar store on Main Street, where her mother worked, and ate a bag of chips, a chocolate bar, and a soft drink, remaining as skinny as a garden hose. Once, her brother shot her out of a tree with a slingshot and she tried to strangle him with a garter snake. We were all in awe of Debbie.

On one end of our block lived the Harrisons with seven spunky daughters and no sons, and across from them the Bubberts, who kept to themselves; and at the other end of the block lived the Barkmans, he a Court of Queen's Bench judge, and across from them lived John Henry and his family. John Henry had a sign-painting business and in the summer he would work in his driveway, creating beautiful signs of all types while the neighbourhood children stood around him in a circle and watched, fascinated. The entire block was used by the children to play games like kick the can, cops and robbers, cowboys and Indians, and arrows, for which I provided the fresh chalk. At six o'clock the siren would go off at the firehall, reminding children all over town to go home for supper, and at nine o'clock it was set off again, reminding them to go home to bed. Saturday nights, the girls had their baths and the next morning we'd all put on our Sunday best and go to church. Sunday dinner was always a beef roast, potatoes, and carrots.

Those were good years. I remember long summer evenings when I would bring ice cream cones to "my girls," as I liked to call them, and thunderstorms when we'd all stand in the front porch, feeling brave and excited and happy.

❧

Have lost my temper with good friend and colleague Miss Hill. Why her, of all people? How long, I said repeatedly, has John Q. Public known about this situation? What situation, Mel? asked Miss Hill. I'd repeat my question. How long has John Q. Public known about this situation? Miss Hill tried to calm me down. Nobody knows, Mel, it doesn't matter anyway what people think . . . I explode: Oh yes it does! *Oh yes it does!* And I repeat the question again and again and again with increasing volume until Miss Hill whispers that she'll be back soon, that I'll be fine, that things will work out, that everybody wants me to be well again, that nobody blames me! Pointless to mention that I blame myself.

*****

Those first five or six years of our marriage were relatively blissful, but there were some chinks in the armour, signs perhaps of another impending breakdown. On Saturdays I would sleep until noon, while Elvira baked the weekly supply of buns and did the banking, racing off to the credit union at ten to twelve before it closed for the day. The odd time she would mention how helpful it would be if I were to take on the banking responsibilities. On Sundays I spent most of the afternoon in bed on an extended meddachshlope (Sunday afternoon nap; some people get an early start on their nap while still in church). Come Monday morning, however, I was raring to go, ready to meet my students and lead them forward through their lessons. My mind spun with ideas for group projects and written assignments, and every morning I eagerly awaited the arrival of my students. I was sowing the seeds of a pattern that would stay with me for life. My reputation as a teacher was growing in the community and so was the number of hours I spent in bed on the weekends. Elvira, in the meantime, was kept busy doing the housework and taking care of Marjorie, born a year and a half into our marriage.

When she asked me if I was okay, I assured her that I was only tired from teaching school all week, and not to worry, I'd be fine after a bit of rest.

One day, shortly after her birth, I sat down and stared at little Marjorie, at her lovely green eyes and black hair, her tiny perfect fingers and her beautiful pale skin, and I told myself that I would always be strong for her, that I was her father, and that I would protect her, as best I could, from harm. I told myself that I would insulate her from the sadness of my past by never speaking of it. I thought I was doing the right thing. I didn't know then that I had made another bad decision. And I took it one step further. I decided on that fateful day that I wouldn't talk to anybody about it, not one single soul. Ever. I had a new home, after all, and a wife and a baby and a career. I was no longer a child, and that part of my life was behind me. After making my decision I felt as though a great weight had lifted. I felt brave and noble, as though I had finally crossed the threshold into manhood.

It was during this time, in my early twenties, that I began to attend church with unrelenting regularity. Not only Sunday-morning service but Wednesday-evening Bible study, Sunday school, and Sunday-evening service too. My favourite hymn is "O for a Thousand Tongues to Sing," an ironic but not unlikely choice for a man who has vowed to keep his mouth shut.

If we were away on holiday the first thing I did when we reached our hotel was inquire at the front desk as to the whereabouts of the nearest Baptist Church (a close enough facsimile of the Mennonite Church) while Elvira asked about restaurants and the kids asked about the pool. Directions to churches were ones I found easy to follow. I must have some sixth sense for feeling out the location of a church. On holidays, I'd get up early Sunday morning, put on my suit and tie, and make my way to church while Elvira and the kids slept late or frolicked in the swimming pool. Church and the classroom became my haven. My faith in God and my faith in my students supplanted any faith I might have had in myself, but I didn't know it at the time. Over the years I was awarded countless certificates for perfect attendance. The congregation would applaud when my name was called yet again, and although I smiled and waved good-naturedly as I bounded up to the front of the church to receive my paper, I always wondered why the normally staid congregation applauded, in the sanctuary no less, and kidded me about it on the church steps as we headed home for our roast beef dinners. Did they think I was doing this to amuse them?

Every morning while shaving I would recite to myself my favourite Bible verses from Proverbs, chapter 3: Trust in the Lord with all thine heart; and lean not unto thine own understanding. In all thy ways acknowledge Him, and He shall direct thy paths.

My paths led to school and church and home. In school and church I gave all of myself, one hundred percent, and so there was very little, if anything at all, left for home. But home, with Elvira and the girls, was safe and private, a warm cocoon outside of the public spotlight where I could collapse and nobody, except Elvira, would know. And I had been brought up to learn that who we are at home and who we are at work and in the community can be as different as night and day.

∾

Remarkably, in spite of her drinking, my mother always managed to get her weekly column, "Pot Pourri," into the local newspaper, the *Carillon News*. Her column consisted chiefly of gossip she'd heard through the grapevine: marriages, deaths, births, graduations, car trips, missionary postings (as opposed to positions), and church news.

Later, my students and I would produce journals and newspapers with similar themes, only having to do with the chock-a-block lives of eleven- and twelve-year-olds.

17

Nurses are outside my room arguing about my clothes. They have lost my underwear in the wash. Why wasn't it labelled? one nurse asks the other. I'll tell the daughters when they come in today, she says. (God forbid!)

He should wear a johnnie (!) because the other patients don't know why he's here. He looks like a doctor when he roams around the halls asking everybody how they're doing. He refuses to wear a gown, she says. Why should he? asks the other nurse, who has as of this moment become my favourite. I wonder, Is this a game? Underwear lost, move back two spaces. Refuses to wear a johnnie, miss a turn. I think next time we play, I'll be the CEO instead of the mental patient.

On August 26, 1963, my father died of stomach cancer, here again, just down the hallway. My brother and my sister and my mother and I were gathered round him for the final time, but he died without saying a word. As in life, so too in death.

On the eve of my father's funeral, Elvira and I made love, and nine months later, here in this hospital in the middle of a record-breaking heatwave, our second daughter, Miriam, was born.

Until then I had been able to manage my illness. I still spent a lot of time in bed on the weekends, and accomplished a great deal at school during the week. I continued to take my medication and see my psychiatrist in the city, an intelligent, soft-spoken gentleman who genuinely cared about me. He was different from the psychiatrist I had seen when I was seventeen. But of course, I told him nothing. The odd time I mentioned that my energy was low on the weekends and high during the week, but that was the only indication I gave that I was still on board the "cockeyed caravan" of manic depression. That he continued to see me month after month, year after year, when I offered him so little to work with, speaks volumes about his commitment and perseverance. Years later when he retired, I felt his loss as deeply as I had the death of my own father. Even if he hadn't been able to help me much, at least he had understood that I needed helping.

We spoke of my childhood in general terms. I told him I had felt lonely as a boy, but no more, nothing untoward, certainly no hint, even, that my mother had been unkind or that I had been criticized often while my brother and sister had not. Or that I was made to work long hours in the chicken barns as a boy or that, when my baby sister died, I was told not to cry and it would soon be forgotten.

My mother lived to be eighty-nine years old and never found the time to put a simple marker on my sister's grave, nor was its location ever revealed to me. Perhaps if I had known more about my mother's past, about her own dark secrets and demons, I might have understood why she was the way she was. I do know that she had been a lively, fun-loving girl from a very conservative background who enjoyed playing baseball with the boys and that it was thought by some that she had been asking for trouble because of it. I do know that in bad periods of drinking she would flail about punching and kicking at the empty air around her, shrieking, in a little girl's voice, the names of various men in the community. Men who are long dead. When my daughter asked her, as an old woman, what she had liked best about her husband, my father, she replied: He was so very gentle.

I did mention to my psychiatrist, at Elvira's insistence, that my mother drank, and he asked me then: Would it have been possible that she couldn't remember, from one day to the next, how she treated you, and so, with your mother as your example, you "forgot" as well?

Naturally I had no answer for him other than to smile and briefly close my eyes.

✏

The birth of my second daughter triggered something inside of me, and I stopped talking at home. I didn't say a word to my wife and daughters for a year. The only sound I made resembled the sounds of abject, wordless grief. Ah, ah, ah, I chanted tonelessly to my infant daughter as I walked her to sleep. At school I was the same as ever: articulate, tireless, enthusiastic, and full of ideas. Around this time I adopted one of the pet expressions I used throughout my teaching career: "Let's try something new." At school I offered encouragement to other teachers, making them laugh at my jokes and impressions, reminding them to keep up the good work. I stocked the cupboards of the staffroom with treats for the teachers and, in the spring, I'd set the long conference table with centrepieces of fresh flowers from my garden. I spent huge amounts of money that we didn't have on gifts for other teachers and extra afternoon snacks for my students. I was eager to please, and Elvira was becoming increasingly alarmed with my erratic spending. Children from lower grades would stop me in the hall and say, Hi, Mr. Toews, can I be in your class when I get to grade six? Marjorie's classmates would tell her, You're so lucky to have Mr. Toews as your dad. I knew every student in the school by name and I made a point of finding out some of their individual interests so that when I greeted them in the hallways I could also ask, for instance, Scored any hat tricks lately, Johnny? or, Hello, Mary, how many books did you devour over the weekend?

If new teachers had recently arrived at the school from elsewhere and if I knew they were feeling lonely or overwhelmed, I would be sure to invite them out to coffee at the Waffle Shop and do my best to make them feel at home. On Christmas Eve, when normal men were hunkering down at home with their families, I was traipsing all over town delivering gifts of ties and socks, which I had purchased from Rieger Clothing, to my male friends and colleagues and boxes of chocolates to my female co-workers. I did this until my retirement, although the list did grow shorter when Elvira reminded me of the cost.

I befriended the custodians (a smart teacher always befriends the custodians) and built shelves for the new library. I organized baseball tournaments and skating expeditions, and every year my students would compete at the provincial music and spoken word festival, performing, with exuberance if not absolute precision, the humorous pieces that we had rehearsed in class. I made sure I had a smile and a kind word for everyone, especially those I thought were feeling down or lost.

On several occasions I would somehow forget that Miriam had been born and I would ask Elvira, Have we had our baby? Then she would take me by the hand and lead me to wherever Miriam was and say, Yes, see, here she is.

There were times when the manic component of my illness

struck me at home, and I came to realize, much later in life, that Elvira dreaded these periods of crazed activity and their inevitable crashing conclusions even more than the depression. My children also came to mistrust my sudden enthusiasm, when I'd eagerly suggest we drive to the city and take in a Jets game or go for a burger at the A&W or play a board game or maybe toss the ball around outside. It was with guarded optimism that they'd agree to play, often only because Elvira encouraged them to do so. During these one- or two-week periods of mania, I'd set not one but two or three alarm clocks for five and sometimes four a.m. and often leap out of bed even before they had rung. Once, Elvira hid the alarm clocks in the basement, hoping, to no avail, that I'd stay in bed a little longer.

I'd spend hours working on the yard and beautifying my flowerbeds, watering, weeding, making them bigger and brighter until the sun came up, and then I'd shower and shave and put on my suit and tie and race off to any number of local coffeeshops, but most often a place on Main Street called Pete's Inn, where I'd chat animatedly with the farmers and businessmen who gathered regularly and often helped Pete the owner by serving endless rounds of coffee, fetching creamers and packets of sugar from behind the counter, and drying the dishwasher-clean cutlery with a tea towel until it shone. From there I'd race to the school and still have a good hour and a half before the students arrived at nine.

I'd use this time to prepare for the activities that I'd planned the night before, setting up various work centres around the classroom, making dozens of trips to the supply room for paper and paint and hammers and nails and whatever else we'd need to bring the textbook to life. Or I would work on the history guide I was writing, called *It Happened in Canada*. I'd greet the teachers as they filtered in through the morning, wishing them well, and then, when the school buses finally rolled in and the town children began to arrive in groups of two or three, I'd stand outside on the sidewalk with my hands on my hips and my shirt sleeves rolled way up, welcoming them warmly and encouraging them to work hard and have a wonderful day.

Only a person who had lived with me for several years, a person such as E., could know that all this "goodness" would soon come crashing down around us like the walls of Jericho.

And that spring of 1964, with the birth of my second daughter, it fell harder than it ever had. Not a word at home for one entire year. Was I angry? Was I, subconsciously, punishing Elvira for her happiness at having another child finally after six frustrating years of trying to get pregnant? Was I insane? Why wasn't my medication working? The pills I took, incidentally, were supposed to keep me somewhere in the middle of my moods, running the gauntlet between depression and mania, but generally leaning towards the safer side of depression. I don't know why the birth of my second daughter, a normally joyous event, would plunge me into darkness and why the birth of my first daughter did not. Did it have something to do with the birth, so many years before, of my younger brother, Reg? When my mother became trapped in a psychotic whirlwind of grief over the death of my sister, of her obsession with her new baby, of maintaining her pious public image, and of her private drinking to quell the ghosts that haunted her?

I had a six-year-old daughter who meant the world to me, and during this time, when she entered my bedroom to tell me about her adventure-packed day, I turned away from her and faced the wall.

At school, however, where she was a grade-one student, I'd smile at her tenderly if her gaze met mine during public assembly and I'd wave to her from across the school playground during recess. After school, if I wasn't staying late to work on some project or another, she and I would walk home together, hand in hand. Perhaps if I was a trained psychoanalyst I could make sense of everything, of the way I was, of the way I so desperately didn't want to be. All I can do is shake my head and wonder how I didn't destroy my family entirely. I suppose I had come, since being born, to associate home with danger and sadness, with the need to take cover, to lie low and hope it all goes away soon. Home, ironically, had become the very cause of my homesickness. I wasn't smart enough to know that our home could be anything different, and yet I knew that I wanted it to be. I wanted to create a happy home but what I really wanted was the memory of a happy home. I was caught in a no-man's land, paralyzed in a place that lay somewhere in between my past and my future, unable to move or dream or call out for help, or even die.

I wanted more than anything for my children to be happy and well cared for, and at the same time their happiness seemed to cut me like a knife. I was envious of my own children's good fortune, of their easy laughter and long, lazy days of play, and most of all of Elvira's abundant love for them and her delight in everything they said and did. The more I resented it, the harder I worked to maintain it. I told myself I would work as hard as I could to provide for them a life of freedom, travel, new clothes, culture, university, whatever their hearts desired. I would work for them and Elvira would be their best friend and confidante. I would make them love me by working hard, by being the best teacher in the world. I should have learned, from my childhood, that hard work guaranteed nothing.

I continued to dream of homelessness two or three times a week, each dream ending in black as though a thick dark dye had been emptied into my brain to blot out everything, every single pinprick of light that may have accidentally filtered into my subconscious, like a small child who wanders into traffic, too young, too beautiful, too precious to be in such a perilous and chaotic place.

18

When *I travelled I was happy.* When I'm with strangers I'm calm and garrulous.

The slant of the sun, the smile of a pretty waitress, birds singing, blue skies, I liked. And perhaps that's why I so rarely allowed myself to leave. I felt that I didn't deserve to relax. Every time Elvira suggested we go on a holiday I'd dig my heels in and come up with excuses for why it was a bad idea. Or I simply wouldn't say a word. After a while she stopped asking me if I wanted to go. She'd simply buy the tickets, book the hotels, take the car in for a tune-up, study the road maps, pack the bags, and inform me that we were ready to go!

My girls have grown up, Elvira is gone, and I'm alone in a hospital room, I don't know whether I'm sad or puzzled or both, awake or dreaming, dead or alive. I'm not sure what I'm doing here. Elvira is dead and I've been in this hospital too long. My girls are working on my case and they will bring me to Elvira. They have told me that everything will be fine again soon. They have told me I will be transferred to the city soon, to where Elvira is, or elsewhere but eventually with Elvira. With home care this time, so she won't get so tired. I don't want to be in the city. I don't want to be in the town. Sometimes I have a great notion to jump in the river and drown. Where I want to be is in my pink house, my dusty rose house at 229 First Street, listening to the sounds of my family in the kitchen, collecting papers for my family file, and that's where I intend to go.

I remember my dusty rose house and Marjorie playing the piano, Schubert's "Largo," the wedding song, and conversation, the phone ringing, Elvira answering Hello! Miriam laughing in a tree outside my bedroom window, jumping onto the roof of the house and scrabbling about like a squirrel, and then . . . her face, upside down, Hello, she's nine years old and peering at me from the other side of the screen, it's summertime, it's warm and her blond hair flops around her grinning face, she's upside down on the roof looking into my room and I'm in bed, and I'm worried she'll fall off the roof, but I don't tell her that, I grin back at her from my bed. Hello there, how's my bomb-shell blonde? I say. Just hanging around, she answers.

✍

That horrible year of silence that began with my daughter's birth and ended twelve months later. Marjorie began to wonder why I never spoke and whether it was because of something she had said or done. Elvira knew that I was in a very rough patch, as they say.

But Marjorie, six years old, remained baffled. I hadn't abandoned my students but I felt that I had abandoned her. At home I sat so quietly at the kitchen table, occasionally looking over at her in her chair, perhaps forcing a smile, but not saying a word.

Elvira did her best to give Marjorie extra attention, but what with taking care of the baby who cried non-stop, and her near catatonic husband, she had little energy left at the end of the day for a small girl who, it seemed, was weathering the situation admirably anyway.

Some afternoons when Marjorie and I were at school and Miriam was finally asleep in her crib, Elvira would run to Mrs. I.Q. Unger's house and cry at her kitchen table the way my father had when Mother's drinking got bad, and the way I had as a boy when I needed to escape Mother's silent anger and disapproval. This time, however, I was the one being cried over, the one being fled from.

It so happened that Mrs. I.Q. lived just a few doors down from us on First Street, so, in the warm summer months when windows were left open day and night, Elvira was able to sit at Mrs. I.Q.'s kitchen table and still hear the angry wails of Miriam when she woke from her nap. Then it would be time for Elvira to dry her own tears and race to the house to tend to our baby, who, perhaps to balance things out, screamed non-stop throughout my year of silence.

And then, as suddenly as it had begun, that horrible year ended. The next spring, when Miriam turned one, I began to speak. And Miriam stopped screaming. Elvira relaxed and made fewer trips to Mrs. I.Q.'s kitchen table, and little Marjorie, in her eighth year, started piano lessons.

I purchased the empty lot behind our backyard and with the stroke of my pen and a few thousand dollars our property doubled in size. The new yard was filled with fruit trees and rose bushes and of course I planted hundreds of red and white petunias as well. I built a sturdy swing for Marjorie and replenished the sandbox for Miriam. I even made a vegetable garden for Elvira, forgetting in the process that she hated rooting in the dirt for food and that she relished her daily trips to Penner Foods where fresh vegetables were cheap and clean and easy to pick at waist level, and where she was bound to meet a friend or two with whom she could enjoy a little spitziring and a good laugh. Mel, she said to me one summer evening as we surveyed our beautiful backyard, I hate gardening with all my heart and soul.

I tried to grow the vegetables myself, but I had little heart for it. I couldn't stop thinking about my flowers, my petunias and tiger lilies and tulips and crocuses and roses and pansies and gardenias and . . . When I woke up in the morning I would rush to the kitchen window to look at my flowers. Just a glimpse of them gave me a feeling of hope and absolute relief, akin perhaps to the feeling a ship-wrecked survivor has when he first spots land in the distance and knows he is saved.

⚬∕∕⚬

That summer we camped with friends (rather pathetically in the rain in a pup tent that covered almost two-thirds of my six-foot-two frame) and had a wonderful time later as we recounted the typical camping horrors of the trip. Miriam learned how to walk, Marjorie fell in love with the piano and provided a rich and progressively less choppy, more polished soundtrack to our lives of Bach and Beethoven, Haydn and Mozart, Schubert and Chopin, and Elvira and I . . . talked!

Oh, what a feeling that can be. A conversation with a beautiful, spirited woman in a yard filled with hundreds and hundreds of life-affirming flowers and two happy children frolicking about! Call me old-fashioned, but that summer I was in heaven. I was a whole man finally, a normal person. The two warring factions inside my head had reached a tentative agreement, the army generals of Mania and Depression reaching across the great divide of my ravaged mind and shaking hands.

19

And then occurred yet another windfall in my life. I was asked by the local school board if I would be interested in a principal's position at Southwood, another elementary school in town. In addition to my duties as principal I would be expected to teach grade six. The school board informed me that I had built, in a very short time, a solid reputation as an innovative and effective teacher, and that in addition to that I had exhibited the leadership and problem-solving skills necessary for the job of principal. The job would provide new challenges, greater room for innovation, more responsibility, and of course a higher salary. Was I interested?

I was, very much so. Elvira and I discussed the pros and cons of such a move and concluded that it would be a good thing to do, a wonderful opportunity. I was very pleased that I had been considered capable of being a principal, although I had never really harboured any desire to become one and I wouldn't have taken the job if I hadn't also been able to teach in the classroom. A few weeks later I met Mrs. I.Q. outside. I had been teaching Marjorie how to ride a two-wheeler, running back and forth along the sidewalk, reluctant to take my hand off the back of her bike seat. Mrs. I.Q. shuffled out onto the sidewalk and hollered at me. Mel, she said, let go once! I did, and of course Marjorie maintained her balance and that was that, she could ride a two-wheeler. Mrs. I.Q. stepped into a square of sunlight on her front yard and waved me over. Well, Melvin, she said, I hear you're going to be a principal now, pretty big deal, nay? I smiled and shrugged. Who knows? I said, I'll try it. So now you've stopped trying to run away from home? she asked, bending over to yank a few dandelions out of her lawn. Well, I have a new one, I said quietly. That's right, said Mrs. I.Q.

We stood and watched Marjorie ride her bike back and forth. I smiled as much as I could, yelling out occasional words of encouragement. At one point Mrs. I.Q. lifted her hand to wave at Marjorie, and I said, No, no, don't. I was afraid Marjorie would wave back and lose all control. Okay, said Mrs. I.Q., stuffing her hands into her apron, no waving. She punched me lightly on my shoulder and chortled to herself. Well, Melvin, she said, there are lots of ways to run, yo? I suppose so, I said, not sure what she was getting at. I think you're safe now, she said, it's time to stop running. She laughed and punched me on the shoulder again. Right? she said. Right, I replied.

⸙

That fall, I said good-bye to the students and staff at Elmdale, who wished me well and hoped that someday I'd be back, and began my new job at Southwood School. The various ingredients of a happy life were coming together beautifully, I thought. Miraculously, I had found life's easy two-four rhythm. I would have made a Faustian pact to have lived the rest of my days this way. My brother and his family now lived in a different town, where he was busy building a career that would eventually culminate . . . right here! (Like mine!) My sister and her family bounced around the mission field saving Latin souls and occasionally landing in Steinbach for some church-sponsored R and R.

Mother continued to have her bouts of getting drunk on vanilla and to write her gossip column and attend church services dressed with her usual flair, wearing any one of twenty or so fancy hats and always, always perched erectly like a nervous bird on the same pew, a little to the left and up front, year in and year out. Occasionally, when her drinking got very bad, we would take her to the hospital to spend some time drying out. She never, not once, acknowledged that she had a drinking problem or that she'd ever had even one single drink in her life, so these drying-out times were rather awkward for her. Hello! she'd cry out when we came to visit, Hello, hello, hello. If Elvira would attempt to talk to her about the problem, or simply to inquire after her well-being, she'd repeat her simple greeting, Hello! hello, hello, hello . . . Which we knew was her way of saying, Not a word! a word, a word, a word . . . And so we sat at her bedside in total silence, while she lay there grinning from ear to ear, her eyes darting from Elvira to me and back to Elvira, ready to screech Hello! if either one of us dared open our mouths.

Thank goodness for the relative normalcy of Elvira's family. Her brothers and I had a genuine respect for one another. I, for their ability to make money hand over fist, for their unabashed delight in spending it, and for their infectious joie de vivre, and they, for my modest degree of education, my passion for teaching school, and my quiet studiousness. Even our physical appearances seemed to convey our different personalities: the brothers were short, none of them over five foot seven, fat, bald, and handsome in the defiant manner of Mafia overlords. I, on the other hand, towered over them, skinny as a rail, like a sick tree. At that time, before my medication made me puffy, I weighed less than a hundred and fifty pounds.

The brothers knew of my illness but I rather think they regarded it as a natural affliction of the sensitive, bookish individual, and in a strange and simplistic way, they understood. None of them had attended school beyond grade twelve, and if any of them had ever read a book, I'd be shocked to hear of it. Later, in the early seventies, I was a part of the committee formed to establish the first public library in Steinbach, and my brothers-in-law, though they've never in all these years seen the inside of it, thought it was a marvellous idea.

It wasn't easy to convince town council that the people of Steinbach would benefit from a public library. We had requested that the library be housed in the town civic centre, but some of the councillors were concerned about the type of "undesirable traffic" it would attract. We all know about the kind of people who hang around the curling rink, the hockey rink, and the post office. Do we want that type of crowd hanging around in the civic centre? Several councillors chastised our group for misrepresenting ourselves. "You said when you came to us two years ago that you would be happy with anything, the most humble facilities, if only we would let you have a library. Now you are talking about deluxe accommodations." The to-ing and fro-ing between town council and Friends of the Library was duly recorded and published in the *Carillon News*. One editor even admonished town council for treating the Friends of the Library "like deadbeat relatives looking for a handout, rather than concerned citizens working diligently for a much needed community facility."

Eventually, after hitting the streets with petitions and garnering the number of signatures (360) necessary to call for a regional referendum on the library issue, and with much persuasion, and with our agreeing to locate in the old Kornelson

School rather than push for "deluxe accommodation" in the civic centre, even though its original building plan had reserved space for a town library within its walls, we were given the green light. There were four of us who formed the nucleus of the library board and we met twice monthly for more than twenty years, during which time the library grew and thrived and became the busiest, most used in the province.

Teenage girls whispered and bickered and giggled at large oak tables, pretending to be working on school projects. Boys fought with each other over the latest Stephen King novel. Earnest Mennonite historians from the Bible school pored over thick volumes of pioneer life and family genealogies, housewives ran in and out with a few paperback murder mysteries shoved in their purses, young couples kissed furtively in dark corners, children played hide and seek between shelves, conservative senior citizens roamed the aisles hunting for offensive material (Ernest Hemingway, J.D. Salinger, Judy Blume), and through it all the friendly, steely-nerved, tough-as-nails Gladys Barkman, head librarian, kept everybody in line.

೧೧

With my library board responsibilities, my teaching, and my new job as principal of Southwood School, I was a busy man, and as fulfilled as I'd ever be. My dreams of homelessness continued, but I chose to ignore them. There wasn't enough time in the day to brood over dreams. I didn't want to be that type of a person anyway. I wanted to stop navel gazing and meeting with my psychiatrist and obsessing over the past. I wanted to become more like my brothers-in-law, more worldly, more confident. I wanted to accomplish things, create things, make a name for myself. I wanted to become as carefree as Elvira and as wise as Mrs. I.Q. I wanted to be well. I wanted to grow up. I wanted to stop being ashamed of every last thing in my life.

It was during this time that I began to take notes. Every morning and every evening before bed I would jot down what I thought were the key points of effective teaching, of boosting morale among staff members, of being civil, decent, and good. I have boxes and boxes of lined recipe cards with notes to myself on how to live, on how to be a role model, on how to bring the very best out of people, on how to educate, to encourage self-expression, to open minds. I reviewed my lessons at the end of each day like an athlete going over every aspect of his game. What worked, what didn't, what captured the attention of my students, what left them cold, which information mattered, and which didn't. I would cull from these lessons the finest ingredients and over time distill them into one smooth golden recipe for success. I was developing my style and honing my craft. I was utterly obsessed with being the best, the absolute best I could be.

Sometime in 1966, during my first year as principal and teacher at Southwood School, the staff decided to produce a play and I was asked to direct. Naturally I assumed these duties with enthusiasm, obsessive attention to detail, and my characteristic good humour. The play, a romantic comedy that is likely no longer in print, was called "Wanted: A Housekeeper." The gist of the plot is simple. A bachelor requires a maid and proceeds to interview several women for the job. (Remember, the year was 1966.) Every day for three weeks, the teachers and I would meet after school in the multipurpose room for rehearsals. Elvira would occasionally come to watch us practise, leaning up against the wall and howling with laughter at our gaffes and earnestness. Can't hear you! she'd call out to the actors if they were mumbling, or Don't turn your back to the audience! There was a role for a young boy in the play, the son of one of the potential maids, and I recruited Marjorie, who was eight, to play the part. Every day, during those three weeks of rehearsals, she'd run the five or six blocks from

Elmdale School to Southwood School, out of breath and grinning from ear to ear, proud to be playing a part in an adult drama. For the actual performance, which was a huge success and attended by all the teachers and their spouses of the Hanover School Division, she wore a grey wool suit borrowed from one of her cousins.

After the play, when life resumed its normal course, I would invite Marjorie to my class at Southwood School, sit her at a desk, and give her grade six tests to write. She loved the challenge. When she was finished I marked them and gave her a grade. She insisted I make no special exceptions for her age, and even though she consistently came up with marks of 38 percent or 43 percent or perhaps the odd 51 percent, she was thrilled to have been tested at the higher level.

Then the two of us would walk home together, along Reimer, across the parking lot of the Evangelical Mennonite Brethren (or E.M.B.) church, past the cemetery where Elvira's six brothers and sisters were buried in a neat row, and her parents too, and down First Street to our beautiful dusty rose house, where Elvira would greet us cheerfully at the door, a tired grin on her face, Miriam on her hip, and dinner sometimes on the table.

And so two years at Southwood passed. That spring I began thinking about my own rather limited education. In those days a year or two at normal school was all that was required, but I knew that times were changing. I knew that I'd require more education, more than a teaching certificate, to be the best that I could be, and although I was very happy at Southwood and would have been content to remain there forever, I decided I would take a year off and go back to university for my Bachelor of Education.

When I made mere mention of the possibility of moving to Winnipeg and pursuing my education, Elvira jumped for joy and said, Hallelujah — thank you, God! Throughout her life one of Elvira's burning desires has been to move to the city, to live amidst the hustle and bustle, to experience the sights and sounds and concert halls and theatres and restaurants and crowds and festivals and commerce and shops and grit and crime and politics and universities and everything else that a city has to offer.

Let's go! she said. Let's do it! I reminded her that it would only be for a year, that the sole purpose of the move was to further my education, and when that was done we'd move back to Steinbach. Yes, yes, she said, scrambling to find suit-cases and arrange a school transfer for Marjorie.

20

The girls have hired a woman, a private consultant who under-
stands the system, they say, to help them convince the doctors
here that I need to be transferred to a psychiatric facility in the
city immediately. That I have gone for fourteen days without
seeing a psychiatrist. That the psychiatrist who saw me when I
was first admitted retired that very afternoon. (Hmmm, was it
something I didn't say?) But that before retiring he had said I
was a very sick man. Daughters are worried sick, very angry.
This woman will help, they say, she knows how to work the
system. This woman says it is imperative that Elvira remains in
the city, health fragile, needs to rest. Elvira unsure. Enraged
with treatment, furious with Bethesda, says if it comes to dying
or being treated at Bethesda, let her die. Will have a stroke if
she talks to one more Steinbach doctor. Wonders why she is
not listened to re her own husband. (Still a fire under that grey
thatch.) Wife and daughters in city: transfer husband. To them.
Have lost track of details re my health, transfer, this hired

woman. Woman says Elvira must not return to house. Or they will let me go home to her, will kill her. Must have help. Is not listened to. Must have home care. Failed kitchen test. Elvira wants me in the city. Girls want me in the city. Fourteen days, they say, fourteen days! Have signed several documents, girls tell me it is the right thing to do. No idea. Write it down.

✒︎

On that spring day in 1968 when Elvira jumped for joy, my plan was hardly a reality. I still had to convince the school board that it was a good idea and ensure that my job would be there for me at the end of the year. Several days later I met with the board and they were all in agreement.

Elvira found an apartment for us on Grant Avenue, across from the new swimming pool built for the 1967 Pan-American games. She signed the kids up for swimming lessons and signed herself up for an aquatic exercise class in her never-ending (and unnecessary) quest to lose ten pounds. I registered at the University of Manitoba, Marjorie was enrolled in grade five for the following September at Rockwood Elementary School, on Rockwood Avenue, just a stone's throw from our apartment, and Miriam, four years old and born restless, was more than ready for a change.

Coincidentally, my sister, Diana, and her family were home on furlough and needed a place to stay. Elvira and I agreed that they could live in our house for a nominal rent while we were in the city. I wrote down elaborate instructions for the care of my flowers and shrubs and left them with my brother-in-law, hoping and praying he'd follow my directions.

Elvira bid a fond farewell to her multitude of friends, insisting that they come to the city and visit, and I promised Mother we would call and see her often. On the way to the city, Elvira hummed and whistled and clutched at my wrists as

I drove, telling me over and over how happy she was to be moving to the city, and Miriam scrambled back and forth from the front seat to the back, to the front, to the back, while Marjorie remained quietly in her corner filled with a mixture of anticipation and apprehension.

The year proved to be an unmitigated disaster. Somehow I managed to complete my degree, limping gamely towards the end of my courses, dragging my body out of bed to attend classes, writing my essays in manic fits and starts as Elvira urged me on, and collapsing, literally, on the finish line, unable to move or even think.

It was a complete nervous breakdown, similar to the one I experienced when I was seventeen. The mania that had propelled me forward for the last few years had now pushed me right over the edge, and I fell and crashed, in spite of all of the medication that was supposed to keep me on the straight and narrow, and in spite of my long-suffering psychiatrist's attempts to get me to talk, to figure me out, to balance my chemicals, and to prevent me from losing my mind.

I was hospitalized for ten days at the Concordia Hospital, during which time Elvira and the girls packed up our belongings between visits to me in the psychiatric ward, cancelled their lessons at the pool, and said good-bye to the few friends they had made in the city.

In addition to missing her friends and suffering the indignity and mind-numbing boredom of having been placed in a slow-learners' class, something we were unaware of until the end of the term, Marjorie was also involved in a bizarre assault right outside our apartment block. One winter evening, on her way home from a church activity several blocks away, she was stopped on the sidewalk by two men, one of whom was carrying a white pail, who asked her for directions to a certain place in the city. She told them she didn't know where it was, and as she turned to enter our building the man with the pail dumped its contents over Marjorie's head. The men fled and Marjorie, shocked, terrified, and humiliated, appeared at our apartment door looking as though she'd fallen into a tar pit.

We never did find out what the mysterious brown substance was. It stained her woollen winter coat and her white furry hat, but it didn't have much of an odour and it washed off her skin easily. In hindsight I realize that we should have phoned the police immediately and had the substance examined. We should have taken Marjorie to a doctor to make sure this awful brown sludge wouldn't harm her. We should have done more. As Elvira comforted Marjorie long into the night, lying beside her in her small twin bed, stroking her brow, murmuring words of love and sympathy, and finally falling asleep with Marjorie cradled in her arms, I lay in my bed blaming myself and wondering what had become of the man who had promised his infant daughter that no harm would ever come to her. It was my fault, I determined. If I hadn't been so eager to obtain a university degree, in order to further my own career, in order to make more money, in order to succeed, in order to provide and impress, in order to feel good about myself, my daughter would not have been violated. In my mind I came to associate the city with evil, despair, and personal failure.

Nor could I acknowledge that I had, in fact, accomplished my goal of getting a university degree, or that the city had offered many exciting opportunities to Elvira, or even that it had been, say, an "interesting experience." All I saw was darkness, and I longed to return to the comfort and familiarity of my hometown and my job at Southwood School. Originally Elvira and I had planned to move back home in June, when Marjorie's school year at Rockwood was over, but in light of the circumstances, we agreed that we would go home the day after my last class and I would return to the city to write my final exams.

Again Elvira packed the boxes and made the necessary

arrangements, dealing with the leasing agency, transferring Marjorie back to her school in Steinbach. Marjorie was ecstatic and relieved to be going home to her friends and classroom. She hollered out instructions to the piano movers as they hauled her prized possession down three flights of stairs and into their truck, on its way back to its rightful place in the pink house on First Street.

There was, however, one small glitch. Diana and her family would not be leaving the house, our house, until June. That was the plan, after all, and whose fault was it that we had returned early if not mine? Elvira and I arranged to live in the parsonage of the E.M.B. church, which just happened to be vacant at the time. Marjorie, wishing not to inconvenience Diana by showing up daily to play her piano, made the trek across town to her aunt Mary's house instead, where she was allowed to play to her heart's content.

I had believed, of course, that I would be back at Southwood in the fall, and if there was anything that had gotten me through my period of depression in the city, it was that.

But I was informed, shortly after moving back to town, that my contract at Southwood would not be renewed, in spite of their verbal agreement to the contrary. I realized that the school board, hearing of my breakdown and my hospitalization, had lost confidence in me, perhaps not as a teacher but certainly as a principal whose job it is to keep everything running smoothly, whose job it is to be reliable. And one doesn't run an elementary school from one's hospital bed.

❧

There's a verse in chapter 16 of Job: I was at ease, but he hath broken me asunder: he hath also taken me by my neck, and shaken me to pieces, and set me up for his mark. Years earlier, my psychiatrist had used the same words to describe me: Mel, he said, you're a mark. Suffice to say, I'd never work as a principal in that town again. Or in any town, for that matter. But I did, eventually, get my house and flowers back. And that fall, I started where I had left off years ago, teaching grade six at Elmdale Elementary. They had always hoped I'd return.

There's a verse in Psalm 16: Thou wilt show me the path of life: in thy presence is fullness of joy; at thy right hand there are pleasures for evermore. This is the verse I chose to underline in my Bible that summer and recite to my reflection every morning as I shaved. In order to maintain a positive attitude, to get out of bed every weekday morning and do my job, I told myself that, if nothing else, God loved me, and that by being good, by being decent and civil and by working hard, I would one day experience the fullness of joy.

Never, ever did I admit or acknowledge even to myself that I was sick. My lapses into depression, I felt, were due to a weakness in my character, and my disappointments and failures in life, though they were rather typical of any average life, were what I felt I deserved. And so I resolved, with steely determination, to become a better human being.

∽

That summer I spent hundreds of hours preparing my classroom for the fall, enlivening it with colourful paint and plants and cushions and curtains and posters and supplies, researching aspects of Canadian history and politics that I had previously overlooked, brushing up on my math (my least favourite subject), planning assignments, group projects, field trips, seating orders, and study guides. Every evening and late into the night I read and reread the biographies of great men and women, hoping to learn something about living one's life to the fullest and leaving one's mark (as opposed to being one) on this

Earth. I filled boxes and then filing cabinets of notes to myself on living and teaching, and in no time the lines between the two subjects blurred. Living was teaching. Teaching was my life.

I didn't just want to be a good teacher. I wanted to be a great teacher, and in order to become one, I felt I had to act as a filter. That is, I had to absorb the negative energy in the classroom, the hurt, the sadness, the confusion in my students. Whatever it was that blocked the mind from understanding, from absorbing information, and from experiencing the exhilaration of learning.

When I returned to Elmdale I was on fire. As I would be for the rest of my teaching days. At home, of course, unless I was manic, I rested. Marjorie was now in grade six and I was her homeroom teacher, a situation requiring some delicacy in how we treated each other, as student, daughter, teacher, or father. But generally it worked out well. Marjorie was a conscientious, clever, well-liked student. In fact, she was one of my brightest students ever, but I waited until she was almost forty before I told her as much. We tended to stay out of each other's way as much as possible. Sometimes her presence would startle me. I would look up from my desk and see her staring at me with those large green eyes she inherited from yours truly and I'd wonder what she was thinking.

That year, too, Miriam began kindergarten at Elmdale and not surprisingly caused some trouble in the classroom by refusing to nap at naptime and by hurling crayons around the room rather than holding them to her paper. She hated cutting, gluing, colouring, napping, and sitting still. Often she was forced by her teacher to stand between the sinks as punishment. Sometimes, if I happened to be at that end of the school, I would peek through the window of her classroom door and watch her. Almost always she would be talking out of turn, whispering, giggling, inciting her friend Debbie into various acts of five-year-old hooliganism. I would see her at assembly occasionally and she would remind me of Elvira in that old kindergarten photo I was telling you about, elbowing her way to the front row, determined to see and be seen.

❧

My daughter has just informed me that it would be good for me to sit outside by the fountain, and that she will sit with me. (It is a dangerous fountain, I presume, one not to be faced alone.) But still, I like the idea. We're off!

We sat in the sun and talked about the kids for a while. We talked about the town. There's no place I can go here, I said, without people seeing me, and talking . . . Until I realized that I wasn't really going anywhere anyway. I tried not to talk about Elvira, knowing how tiresome it was for my daughters to continuously reassure me that she was alive and in the city. But I couldn't help myself. You'll see her soon, she says. She desperately needed a break, she says. We're taking care of her in the city and you here, and it doesn't make sense. But she's getting stronger. She wants to see you. We're making progress. Progress? I ask. Yes, she says, we've got an appointment for you in the city to see a geriatric psychiatrist. (Horrifying words those: they mean I am old *and* crazy.) Then, daughter goes on to say, the ball will be rolling and we can get you home care with Mom in the city and access to better care, but you have to be in the city to qualify for . . . I drifted away. I had a frightening feeling that my daughters were only somewhat less confused about the situation than I was.

We sat outside for about an hour. I was beginning to get a nice suntan, and my daughter recommended a certain type of sunscreen to prevent skin cancer. I'll be fine, I told her, not to worry. The sun likes me. A former student and his wife walked past us and we chatted for a minute or two. He introduced me to his wife, and I introduced him to my daughter. When they leaned over to shake hands, the fountain suddenly erupted and they both got a little wet. Did my former student wonder what I was doing sitting by the hospital fountain? Or did he already know?

When we came back inside my daughter kissed me good-bye, and I noted that warm, earthy summer smell on her skin, which reminded me of the lake, of our cottage, of her as a little girl, and of myself as something other than old and crazy.

It's time to rest, the nurse says. Does she think sitting by a fountain is hard work?

Overheard nurse at desk telling other daughter on the phone: I wouldn't get any nursing done if I was forever looking for your dad. My lunch has been forgotten. The places that I go: bed, washroom, hallway, now the fountain. Where has she been looking?

21

Three good years went by. I worked, the children went to school happily and spent time with their friends, and Elvira kept house. Mother had begun to shoplift her bottles of vanilla now, lining her large purse with tea towels so the bottles wouldn't clink. This was also the time I began to take very long walks. Soon I was wearing out a pair of shoes per month, and Elvira insisted I buy better-quality walking shoes.

In the summer I gardened and researched the lives of remarkable men and women while Elvira feverishly planned road trips, sitting up in bed with maps and travel brochures, a bowl of popcorn, and the ball game blaring on the television that we had recently purchased. Elvira's passion was baseball. Most of our trips included visits to cities that had major league teams, Elvira having bought tickets in advance over the phone, and not for one game but for three or four, including afternoon games. She'd insist on arriving an hour or two early for the experience of watching the players warm up and of collecting their autographs. In the last few years, as her baseball passion soared to a near hysteria, Elvira built herself a wall map of North America and marked, with a coloured thumbtack, every city in which she had seen a game. In fact, she developed a three-colour system: red for the cities she has visited with the girls and me, yellow for the cities she has visited with her baseball-loving friend Miss Martha Hill (the one I lost my temper with) and my grandson, and blue for the cities she has visited alone.

When Elvira wasn't watching — or reacting to, I should say — the baseball game, or taking in an episode of *M.A.S.H.* or *The Waltons* or *McMillan and Wife*, I would watch *Hymn Sing*, my favourite show, although I was almost equally as fond of *Front Page Challenge*, with its inimitable panel of regular guests, Pierre Berton, Gordon Sinclair, and Betty Kennedy, and affable moderator, Fred Davis. *Hymn Sing* aired at 5:30 on Sunday evenings and preceded *The Wonderful World of Disney*, Miriam's favourite show after *Don't Eat the Daisies* and *The Secret Life of Walter Mitty*. *Hymn Sing* consisted of a formally dressed Winnipeg choral ensemble standing rather stiffly on strategically placed risers and singing hymns. The lyrics of the hymns, for those who weren't familiar with them and wanted to sing along, rolled along the bottom of the screen.

It was becoming clear that Elvira was longing for something else. Not something instead of what she had but something in addition to it, something that I was oblivious to. So when it happened I was floored.

No, she didn't have an affair or leave town one day to become a hippie in Kathmandu or some such place. Elvira cashed in her life insurance policy, purchased by her father when she was an infant, bought herself a flute, and joined the local orchestra, under the tutelage of the talented Bill Derksen.

In those days Mennonite women did not perform in public. They weren't even allowed to get up and speak to the congregation, although fifteen-year-old boys were. The role they were expected to play was strictly behind the scenes, at home, in church, and in the community. So when Elvira took up the flute and joined the band I saw it as an act of rebellion, of defiance, not only of the Mennonite way but of me, or of the man I felt I was supposed to be, although my bewilderment left me, naturally, speechless. Never would it have occurred to me to ask her to stop or even to ask her why she felt she needed to join an orchestra. Every Tuesday evening, Elvira would leave the house at seven, her narrow black case tucked protectively under her arm, for two hours of orchestra practice with the illustrious maestro. She loved to say the words "orchestra practice."

It wasn't long before Marjorie, naturally gifted when it came to music, had bought her own flute (that life insurance policy was coming in handy) and joined her mother in the band. Elvira had sewn each of them a long black dress for performances, and the two of them spent hours sashaying around the house in their regulation show gear, spontaneously performing mini-concerts on the flute for Miriam and me, after which we dutifully applauded and asked for more. And then, as if our family wasn't making enough of a joyful noise unto the Lord, Elvira roped Miriam into learning the violin (purchased of course with the life insurance money) and joining the junior orchestra! In no time Elvira and the girls were banging out the classics on piano, flute, and violin every Sunday after roast beef, while I, now an audience of one, sat in my La-Z-Boy straining to recognize the melody beneath all the clatter. More often than not a squeak or a toot not written into the music would reduce Elvira and the girls to tears of laughter and at that point I would smile, stand up, and announce my necessary departure, either to my bedroom or to my flowers in the backyard.

I did, as the girls improved, come to relish these Sunday

afternoons. Often, I would ask them to play and sing, and they would happily indulge me. Marjorie, by now a virtuoso on the piano, could play just about anything, but Miriam preferred to sing the sad French songs of Jacques Brel. Wearing her Pioneer Girls tam as a beret and holding a chopstick for a cigarette, she would beg her sister to play them over and over and over again to the point where I began to worry about her frame of mind. Another of her favourites, oddly, was the "Notre Dame Victory March," written by the Reverend Michael J. Shea, which she would belt out with such earnest heartfelt gusto that both Marjorie and I had to hide our laughter.

⚬◞◟⚬

Something about the flute incident tweaked my brain and made me realize that I too could take up a hobby, that my life of work and sleep was too narrow, that I was missing out on things, and that it was okay to have a little fun from time to time. And so I approached the possibility rather tentatively and with not a small amount of fear.

In previous years we had enjoyed summer vacations in a town called Falcon Lake, eighty miles from town near the Manitoba-Ontario border, usually renting a cottage from a lakeside resort by the name of Big Buffalo Cabins. One summer Elvira idly mentioned that the prices of cottages in the area were down and that really if we were going to be renting a cabin at Big Buffalo every summer, it made as much sense to simply buy our own and come and go as we pleased. That very afternoon the girls and Elvira and I packed up the Ford Custom 500 (all of our married life I stubbornly insisted on driving Fords, to the chagrin of Elvira, who prefers Oldsmobiles and Lamborghinis) and headed for the South Shore to have a peek at the cottages up for sale.

I'll never forget that gorgeous June afternoon as we slowly

wound our way along the gravel roads of cottage country, pointing out the cottages we liked (lots of windows!) and the ones we didn't (haunted!) while the girls chattered excitedly about the things they'd do at the lake, the friends they'd have sleep over, with Elvira bemused in the front seat next to me, smiling, touching my arm, reminding me that life could be grand. This makes you happy, doesn't it? she'd ask, her feet up on the dash, hand tapping the roof of the car.

And it did. Oh boy, did it ever! Eventually we settled on a small, modest pink affair (always pink) on the top of a hill with a woodburning stove, an outhouse in the back, a large front yard for badminton and barbecuing, and three bedrooms, one of which had a built-in double bunk bed that could sleep six little girls at a time. It was not a lakefront property but we had our own dock in the bay just on the other side of the road and down a narrow path, a minute's walk away. The year was 1971 and the cottage cost us $7,000.

That summer I bought a red fibreglass canoe for Elvira for her birthday, and the two of us, and sometimes the four of us, would paddle around our bay after supper, listening to the loons and the motorboats and the distant voices of other cottagers and wondering, at least I was, what I had done to deserve such happiness. We still went on road (baseball) trips in the summer (stopping at every single historical marker along the way so that I could jump out of the car and copy its message word for word into my notebook, much to my daughters' exasperation). But now, instead of simply going home afterwards, we could go to the lake. It remains one of the few places in this world, if not the only place, where I was able, truly, to relax. When you're a schoolteacher, and especially when you're a teacher in a small town, you are on stage nearly all the time. It is inevitable that you will, on a daily basis, run into students, former students, and parents of students, and you are expected to be a constantly cheerful, supportive, reliable pal to all of them, forever. Not that I resented having to be such a person — that was exactly the sort of man I wanted to be, the type of level-headed, upbeat individual I most respected and admired. But oh, the fatigue of it.

22

I have made another mistake. I have mixed up words, again. Am beginning to panic, as though I'm running out of oxygen. What have I left? Not what have I left, but what do I have left? is what I'm trying to say. Mistake re the word "confusion": nurse enters room, checks my feet, mentions something about contusion on foot, to which I respond, Yes, it seems I can't make head nor tails of things. I actually wonder what my foot has to do with my confusion and say so. Really, I say politely, it has to do with my head. Nurse responds: Your feet? I answer: My head. Nurse says: Mel, we are talking about your feet right now, okay? Inane conversation, non-conversation. Yes, let's talk about my feet, why not? The nurse eventually left, and my daughter entered, with more paper, fancier than legal, but why? I know why. It is because she feels it is all I have, paper, and so she's . . . Before we could greet each other conventionally, I said, in a loud, panicky voice, Good. You're here. Now, help me with a few things. Let's get a few things straight. Sit down.

Here's a pen. Now write it down, please. Write this down: I will be well again. I will see Elvira again. I am not ill.

I think I have frightened her. She is looking at me strangely, but she is writing it down. I will be well again, she writes. I will see Elvira again. I am not ill.

But then, if I am not ill, what am I? Why am I here? I ask her. Modification: she tries again. I am ill, but I will get well again. I will be fine, I will be healthy soon. She hands me the fancy sheet of paper with these words on it, and I look at it. It is not sufficient, but somehow I manage to smile and thank her. Forgive me, I say, the lights are . . . I nod, she knows, and she begins to cry. She leaves, telling me she is getting coffee, returns smiling. Just write down the things you remember, she asks me cheerfully. Please?

∽

The year was 1972. Marjorie — or Marj, as she started to be called around then — was fourteen, Miriam was eight, my siblings were living in the States and overseas, busy in their respective helping fields of social work and missionary zeal, and Elvira and I were both thirty-seven years old. The next four years, as I recall, were good ones, discounting my continuous internal struggles with manic depression compounded by my utter refusal to talk about it with any living soul.

My efforts at school, in the public library, and in church were noticed and appreciated by the community at large. My reputation as a teacher was growing in leaps and bounds, and although I still harboured a desire to be a principal, I was more than content in the classroom.

At home, I was the same, and more so. I was distant, silent, and sad much of the time. Elvira was, in almost all respects, functioning in the role of a single parent, and my relationship with my daughters, what there was of it, began to falter. When they were babies I could hold them in my arms and sing to them and when they were little children we could play rather than talk, but as they grew up I lost my footing as a father. I didn't know how to be with them, other than as a teacher, and the odd time I made an effort to interact casually and affectionately as I felt a father should, it felt forced and artificial and I knew they sensed it too, and I became self-conscious. I retreated into my bedroom, reassuring them with a few words of my love and concern, and smiling at them often like a distant relative, unsure how to proceed from there.

I didn't know how to respond to their joy or to their easygoing everyday banter, but when the chips were down for them I reached out. If nothing else I understood their sadness, so when they were sick in bed or disappointed, or even heartbroken, I found it so much easier to act as a father should, offering words of encouragement and sympathy, and making stabs at goofy, light-hearted repartee.

At about that time, when she was eight or nine, Miriam bought a poster for herself and glued it (in the future Elvira and I recommended the use of scotch tape for such things) to her bedroom wall. The picture was of a kitten hanging from a wash line by its two front paws, and under it the caption Hang in There, Baby! Whenever Miriam was feeling blue or overwhelmed, I would remind her (and of course myself) of that message. Hang in there, baby! was one of the few things I actually said to her, and lately she's been saying it quite a lot to me, trying to get me to smile, which I do. The other day we said it to each other at the very same time, and laughed.

When she was ten years old the concept of open-area teaching came into vogue, and our school board decided to knock out the walls between the two grade five classes and the two grade six classes. I was very much opposed to the idea of blackboards on wheels being used instead of walls between the classes. What will I do? I asked Elvira after I'd been told my walls were coming down. You'll adjust, she said, you'll manage. (Want some ice cream?) My classroom was a noisy one, generally because I was so fond of group projects and dramatizations and hammering and sawing and just maintaining a healthy hum of ideas and opinions that I had no idea how we'd manage in an "open area."

One thing I discovered, however, while coping without proper walls, was the amount of trouble Miriam was getting into at school. She was in grade five, in the classroom directly next to mine, and now, thanks to the open-area concept, I could hear much of what was going on over there. From what I could tell she did a fair amount of visiting, laughing, and interrupting others, particularly the teacher, with ridiculously impertinent questions and flippant remarks obviously meant to amuse her friends. I never mentioned to her that I could hear her acting up in class, because I wasn't supposed to have heard this in the first place and because I didn't want to meddle in the affairs of her teacher.

In the meantime I tried to stay away from the blackboard on wheels and closer to the front of my class, where I wouldn't hear what was going on in hers. Once, when I had absent-mindedly wandered to the back, Miriam, who had noticed my large shoes on the other side of the blackboard on wheels, leaned over, poked her head under the blackboard, and said, Hi, Dad!

One time, however, I sensed that she had crossed over the line into bad behaviour. From what I could ascertain, through the blackboard walls, she had placed a thumbtack on a student's chair, a boy she had clashed with several times already. He had shot out of his seat yelling and had disturbed the class, which infuriated his teacher. Who is responsible for this? said Miriam's teacher. Nobody in her class said a word, and I moved a little closer to the blackboard, eager to know how it would all play out. Again, her teacher asked the question, Who is responsible for this? I was so nervous. I didn't want Miriam to think she could put a tack on somebody's seat whenever she felt like it, but I also didn't want her to get caught. Finally, she was turned in by an honest classmate with noble intentions and marched out of the classroom into the main hallway where her teacher would be sure to give her a very stern talking to and some type of assignment befitting the crime, not to mention a command to apologize to the boy in front of the entire class.

After what seemed like hours, I heard her shuffle back into the classroom, sniffing, repentant, and humiliated. I felt so bad for her that I made up an excuse, on the spot, to go to the library. The only way of getting to the library with our ill-conceived open-area concept was to walk directly through Miriam's classroom, while keeping close to the barrier so as not to be too disruptive. As I walked past Miriam's desk, I reached out my hand and mussed her hair gently, and was gone.

That evening during supper Elvira asked the girls how their days had gone, and Miriam, after returning my smile from across the table, answered, Good! This rare connection between the two of us sustained me for days.

❧

Down First, up William, across Main. Across Main, down William, up First. Day after day after day after week after week after month after month after year after year after year. I taught school. I was a schoolteacher. I believe that's correct.

❧

I remember playing baseball with my students and hitting twenty-seven foul balls in a row that, if they had been straight, would surely have been spectacular home runs. There I stood at home plate, my tie tucked in between the buttons of my shirt, my sleeves rolled up, a good-natured grin on my face, primed for a grand slam, and knocking twenty-seven fouls into the stands. I hit fouls consistently. One day Mrs. I.Q. was walking past the school as the kids and I played baseball. I was at bat, and hitting fouls, and Mrs. I.Q. yelled out, Straighten 'em out, Mel, you're waiting too long!

My tentative approach to hitting the ball extended into my social life as well. Elvira and I were a part of a group made up of four couples. The men in this group, all of them except me, were spirited, outgoing, argumentative, and loud, and I loved to get them going on one subject or another, usually political or economic. I would casually allude to an issue, for instance the building of a new hockey arena, something I knew would fire them up, and then I would sit back with a satisfied grin as they took the bait, arguing passionately, explosively, and sometimes even eloquently, for hour after entertaining hour. If there was a lull in the debate all I had to do to get them going again was mention Trudeau's name, and they'd be off and running like a pack of dogs to a single bone. Elvira would also take part occasionally, grateful for the opportunity to lay down her paring knife or whatever it was she was wielding in the kitchen with the other wives and enter the fray in the living room. She and I would wink conspiratorially at each other as she joined in the discussion with her left-of-centre political opinions, a surefire guarantee for getting these conservative Mennonite businessmen even more riled up than before.

23

In 1976, my small world turned upside down when I lost my home again and this time for good. Steinbach was growing quickly in those days and businesses were vying for space on Main Street as they expanded to accommodate the growing population. Our house on First Street sat directly behind a busy Ford dealership. Steinbach was establishing itself as "The Automobile City," and folks came from all over the province for good deals on a new car.

Albert Enns at this dealership needed my property to expand the business and remain a competitive force in the automobile industry. At first he approached me indirectly. Hey, Mel, have you ever given any thought to selling? Of course I hadn't. I had built this home from scratch and nurtured the yard and flowerbeds and fruit trees and maple trees into a veritable Garden of Eden.

Several weeks later, Albert Enns made an offer, a low one, and I told him again that I had no intention of selling. And then Albert said he would propose a zoning amendment to town council that, if passed, would have the block in which my house stood zoned commercial as opposed to residential, which would mean we were out and he was in. Who knows if he would have done it, but it scared me, and I retreated. Elvira encouraged me to call his bluff, or to just plain ignore him, and stop worrying about it. But I was absolutely stricken, paralyzed with fear at the possibility of appearing in court, of violating a zoning code.

I decided to move. The realtor kept coming around, trying to get me to lower the price, and, after I relented, turned around and sold the property to Albert. He got the house and property and, over the course of the next few years, expanded his dealership according to the plan he had drawn up even before I had agreed to sell. Eventually he had my house removed entirely, carted off to the country, and had the basement filled in. Today bright shiny new cars mark the spot that had been our home, and my most important accomplishment.

Elvira and I and the girls moved to a new white brick bungalow with a double garage, wall-to-wall carpeting, a finished basement, two fireplaces, three bathrooms, a sauna, and a large yard. A nice home, a lovely home in fact, quite luxurious from all appearances. Our new address was 58 Brandt Road, and it was only two or three hundred yards, across a field and past a few houses, from our old house. Often I would sit in my new fancy living room and stare out the picture window at the pink house at 229 First Street, wondering what had happened, wondering why I had let it happen. Occasionally I would walk past it, when I was feeling brave, and chart its progress of decline. Albert had rented it out to a young family for the length of time it would take him to develop the land around it. The screen on the front door became torn, the paving stone on the little walk leading up to the house was chipped off, and the flowers hadn't been replanted or the windows washed or the eaves cleaned or the lawn mowed regularly or the driveway properly shovelled.

Years later, after the house had been removed, Albert Enns met me on the street. That's business, he said with a good-natured shrug, as if to indicate his helplessness in the matter. Don't worry about it, Albert, I said cheerfully, what's done is done. Three weeks later, in a complete and regrettable act of madness, I bought a car from him, in an attempt to remove any trace of hard feelings he might think I had for him. Elvira had, long ago and for her own self-preservation, learned to laugh at my foibles, rather than become exasperated, and I was grateful for it. We had, it seemed, a tacit agreement not to call each other on points of "strange behaviour" and simply to move ahead, hoping, hoping for normalcy.

This move marked the very beginning of the end of my world as I knew it. There were other factors as well. It was the mid-seventies and even Steinbach was changing, albeit slowly, with the times. Which reminds me of a joke: How many Mennonites does it take to change a lightbulb? Answer: Change?

Elvira by this time was attending the School of Social Work at the University of Manitoba, commuting in car pools made up of women Marj's age. Forty-year-old Mennonite housewives from Steinbach did not, as a rule, attend university, and Elvira naturally enjoyed being one of the first to do so. Marj was studying history at the university, living in the city in an apartment she shared with friends, and coming home on the weekends. Miriam had begun grade seven at the Steinbach Junior High School. (And had, thus far, avoided suspension.)

My family had changed, but I remained the same. The only thing that was different was that now, rather than going down First, up William, across Main, I was going down Brandt, up William, and across Main. And back. And forth. And back and forth, becoming more bewildered with every heavy step, and more determined than ever to hide it from everyone.

Just ran into a former student visiting her grandmother. She called to me from down the hall. I recognized your walk, she said, laughing. It's very distinctive. I remembered that I had, in fact, fashioned my style of walk to conceal my depression. I would not, I reasoned at the time, be accused of dragging my heels, or of shuffling along the streets of Steinbach in some kind of despondent funk.

Are you visiting somebody here, Mr. Toews? asked my former student when we had finished chuckling about the past. Yes, I said, still smiling, that's right, that's right. I'm just out for a walk and I thought I'd pop in and visit a friend. My student said, So you're keeping busy, then, are you? Absolutely, I said in my booming classroom voice, and enjoying it.

I hoped the nurse on duty wouldn't come and ask me to return to my room.

You were my favourite teacher, you know that? stated the woman. And you were my favourite student, I quipped. I remember the day you ran into the teeter-totter and chipped a tooth. You were very brave about it. I recall there being quite a lot of blood.

Was I? she asked. That's funny, I still have it. And she smiled, with exaggeration, so that I could see the chipped tooth. I better be going, she said. Take care of yourself, Mr. Toews. I will, I said, and you too. And give my regards to your husband, I added. He had also been my student. Is he still interested in becoming the prime minister?

She laughed and shook her head. No, no, she said, he's working for his dad in the shop, welding. Well good for him, I said, if I need any welding done in the future I'll know where to go . . .

You bet, said my student, and we smiled yet again and waved and waved, and then she was gone.

❧

Spent several moments staring at "Summer Memories," reflecting, and flipping through book of poems. References to trains: many. Interesting for a boy who grew up in a town without a station. Reason: Elders afraid of outside world influences shipped in by train. Nearest depot: Giroux, Manitoba.

❧

The move to a new house, my girls growing up, my wife broadening her horizons: Shortly after moving to Brandt Road, Elvira began planning our trip to South and Central America. In a year's time, we would be visiting our friends Stan and Marion Houghton in Pifo, Ecuador, near Quito, where Stan worked as a radio technician, and also, briefly, my sister and her family in Panama City. When I voiced some concern over the cost of this trip, Elvira told me that she had, that day, taken a job as a receptionist at the chiropractor's office (in addition to more social work classes at the university) and that every paycheque she received would go into our South American fund. Try not to worry, Mel, she said excitedly, it'll be great! You'll have lots to write about!

I looked forward to our adventure with a combination of intense, palpable dread that affected my bowels and minimal, fearful curiosity. Didn't they shrink heads in Ecuador? I may have been weary of living in my own turbulent head but I didn't relish the thought of having it shrunk to the size of a grapefruit and hung from the waist of a naked Ecuadorian Indian man. I knew Elvira would take care of all of the details, the tickets, the immunizations, the malaria pills, my medication, the passports, the travellers cheques, the packing, the travel insurance, the securing of the house while we were gone, and everything else a person has to do in order to ship her family to another continent for six weeks. All I would have to do, on our scheduled day of departure, was get out of bed, get dressed, and get into Elvira's brother's car. He had agreed to drive us to the airport in Winnipeg. Rather a nice and surreal way to leave the country for the summer: Just wake up and go. On the way to the airport I managed to voice my concerns to Elvira: We're not scheduled to visit any headshrinking territory, are we?

She laughed, grabbed my wrists, and said, Of course not!

Marj, her university courses having ended in April, had already left for Stan and Marion's. When the rest of us arrived, after a brief stopover in Bogota, where we were held up by bandits and rescued by the police all in the course of approximately forty heart-stopping seconds, the Houghtons welcomed us graciously into their home, located on a small compound of houses rented out to the radio staff and other assorted missionary types. It was on this beautiful, windswept compound high up in the Andes that Elvira met an Irish woman who taught her how to make French silk pie, a delicious rich dessert that both she and I instantly loved. Frankly I would have been quite content to remain on the compound, staring at the mountains and exchanging recipes with the neighbours. But it was not to be. Elvira had not saved every penny from her receptionist job to come all the way to South America in order to sit around in lawn chairs engaging in idle chitchat with people who weren't even Ecuadorian.

Stan and Marion and their daughter, Becky, who was close in age to Marj, had planned to take us on a meandering road trip in their Land Rover, with overnight stops along the way at various friends' homes in places like Quito, Guayaquil, Rio Bamba, Cuenco, and Banos. Very good! I exclaimed, attempting to sound enthusiastic. Sounds wonderful! Where else are we going? And when do we leave?

Right now, answered Stan, a gentle, affable man who never

seemed to lose his cool. And so we piled into the Land Rover and hit the narrow, rutted, treacherous mountain roads on what was to become a memorable odyssey for all of us. And guess what, Mel? said Elvira, who was beaming in the front seat, elbow out the window, hand tapping the roof of the Land Rover, happy as a clam and drinking in the scenery and the sights like a woman who's spent the last thirty years in a windowless cell. What! I yelled from the back seat, where Miriam and I had stationed ourselves. We are going to headshrinking territory after all!

Of course we were. Fabulous! I answered. Can't wait!

Actually, interjected Stan, the voice of reason, there hasn't been a documented headshrinking in at least four years.

Ah, I said, not documented . . . are they usually?

But of course Stan and Marion and Elvira and Marj and Becky were laughing by this point, and I had come to believe that I wasn't going to survive the trip anyway and that brings a certain sense of calm to a man, in a strange way. I took Miriam's hand and squeezed it and she gave me a reassuring look, a Hang-in-there-baby kind of look, and I smiled back. It hadn't occurred to me that we would all lose our lives on this crazy expedition, only, for obvious reasons, that I would and that the others would return home unscathed.

But of course I kept notes. If my head were to be shrunk, it would be documented, I would see to that, at least.

In my journal I recorded the first verse of the poem by Emily Brontë entitled "Last Lines":

No coward soul is mine,
No trembler in the world's storm-troubled sphere:
I see Heaven's glories shine,
And faith shines equal, arming me from fear.

24

O*ur road trip proved to be a success* filled with laughter, adventure, romance, danger, and excitement, and I meticulously filled several ringed notebooks with the details of the journey. We attended an all-day wedding in a village called Pulucate, high up in the Andes, watching respectfully from our seats on a log in the back of the grassy plateau as the minister, at one point in the proceedings, turned his back to the couple and the audience and urinated off the side of the cliff. After the ceremony, we were ushered into several grass huts where we were served, by the fifteen-year-old bride herself, buns, oranges, salad, and guinea pig. (Elvira tricked me into eating it by telling me it was chicken.) After the wedding we walked for several miles back down the mountain path to the road where the Land Rover was parked, and Elvira picked wildflowers from the side of the road and gave them to me as a present. Marj wound them into a type of headband for me and made me pose for several photographs. Wonderful day in the

Andes Mountains, I recorded later that evening in Notebook Number 3.

Many times, as I have noted, I was afraid the Land Rover would go over a cliff. Around curves, as is the mountain custom, Stan would honk his horn. If there was oncoming traffic, the car on the side nearest the mountain wall had the right of way. The road was wide enough for one vehicle only and the driver on the outside, nearest the sharp drop, would have to back his or her car, sometimes for a mile or two, to a spot in the road that had been widened slightly for the purpose of passing. Why this was the case, that the inside vehicle had the right of way, I do not know, and I wonder how many heart attacks have occurred as a result. Stan was used to driving in the mountains, and if backing up for a mile along curved, narrow dirt roads and risking plunging off thousands of feet into rocky ravines made him nervous, he didn't show it. Many times during these reversing sessions I would glance out the window and see no road beneath me, only the turbulent water far below. One time, during a particularly terrifying reverse, I told Stan I would get out and walk, and he said, Mel, there's no room on the road to walk. Miriam and I, in our usual positions in the back seat, patted one another's hands, exchanged fatalistic grimaces, and waited to die.

Then there was the headshrinking leg of our journey. Somehow we had made it to Shell, a small military base on the edge of the jungle, and, as the name so arrogantly suggests, a town taken over by the large American oil and gas company. From Shell we were to fly to Macuma, a tiny jungle village smack in the very heart of headshrinking territory. Stan and Marion knew of a missionary couple who lived in that village and who would be more than happy to show us around. Excellent, I murmured, have them put the water on to boil.

And so, after a sleepless night of taking cover from the bats that lived in the military barracks in which we stayed and a breakfast of fried plantains, seven of us, including the pilot, piled into a six-seater Cessna and prepared for takeoff. Stan had opted to stay behind in Shell because there wasn't room for all of us, and because they had been to the jungle before. (I too had offered to stay behind, but Elvira told me this would probably be a once-in-a-lifetime opportunity, and I couldn't think of a counter-argument at the time.) The seventh person travelling with us did not take up a seat of his own. He was a baby, the son of one of the Indian jungle-dwellers, and he had been airlifted into Shell for medical treatment. His mother had walked for four days through the jungle to bring him to Macuma, knowing that he was very sick and close to death. The Indians living in the jungle were, probably wisely and very likely with good cause, suspicious of the white missionaries, the doctors, the pilots, and the American oilmen, but this mother had no options at the time other than to watch her son, if not treated, die.

The nurses at the small clinic in Shell had made arrangements with Marion to have this baby travel with us back to Macuma, where his mother would be waiting for him. During the flight Elvira held the sleeping baby, wrapped in a soft yellow blanket, on her lap, and the girls crowded around him, oohing and aahing over his inch-long eyelashes and dark head of hair. When we landed, the baby's barefoot mother was at the door of the airplane within seconds. Elvira handed the woman her son, and she, without a word or any expression whatsoever, tied him to her back and disappeared into the jungle, presumably to begin her four-day journey back to her home. What an act of faith, what an act of love, I thought of her decision to give her son over to foreigners in the hopes that he'd be healed. I wondered what type of resistance to the idea she might have met from other people in her village. I duly noted this experience in my notebook.

Later that day, after a refreshing glass of lemonade at the

home of Marion's missionary friends, we went on a guided walk around the village, which consisted only of a few residential huts, a few more modern homes, such as the one in which the missionaries lived, a tiny landing strip for planes to land with supplies for the villagers, a school hut, and a church hut. The children we encountered were friendly but said nothing, the adults were wary, and I felt profoundly ridiculous for being there. Nevertheless, Mrs. Moroz paraded us around the place and then suggested we go for a hike in the jungle. Of course, I said, and afterwards let's go for a refreshing dip in the piranha-infested headwaters of the Amazon. What are we waiting for?

We weren't as far as a hundred yards into the dense, dark jungle when Miriam got her boot stuck in the muck along the narrow path. Really stuck. Cautiously I crept over a rotten log that spanned a type of greenish, mossy bog to where she stood rooted to the ground and laughing at her predicament. I suggested she take her foot out of the mired boot and balance herself by holding on to my back. Then I leaned over and attempted to tug the boot out of the muck, nearly falling over repeatedly as Marj took photographs and yelled encouraging words to me over the muffled roar of Elvira, Marion, and Mrs. Moroz laughing.

It took ages to remove the boot and in the course of the procedure both Miriam and I became covered in jungle slime, dirt, and offal. Eventually we got the blasted boot out, and Mrs. Moroz, whose white dress had remained spotless throughout, washed our clothes in her primitive ringer washer and hung them up to dry. In the meantime Miriam wore a hilariously uncharacteristic outfit, which she, so hypocritically, refused to be photographed in: a conservative high-necked dress with a small floral print, belonging to Mrs. Moroz, and I wore her husband's housecoat. If the villagers had needed something to laugh at, something to mock, we would have fit the bill nicely.

In any case, I believed, our clown status in the village would prevent our heads from being shrunk. What prestige is there in shrinking the head of an imbecile, after all? A court jester's life is saved by the mere fact that he's perceived as a moron, and so I thought would be mine.

We left Macuma and met up with Stan and Becky in the bat-infested barracks of Shell and drove back towards the teeming, torrid coastal city of Guayaquil. Along the way we had many adventures, though none quite, as nerve-racking as the jungle tour, not counting the shopkeeper from Cuenco who threatened Elvira with a machete for not buying a piece of fabric she had made the mistake of admiring. Marion sorted him out, surprising him into stunned submission by speaking sharply to him in his own language. Elvira loved the fact that she had been threatened by a machete-wielding Ecuadorian.

After spending two weeks in Panama City, with its intriguing canal, and in La Chorerra, where my sister lived, I was ready to leave.

One thing I do remember when I think of Panama: the death of Elvis Presley, on August 16, 1977. I was not a fan of his music but I had been tracking his career haphazardly over the years. Well, not his career, really, but his personal travails. Many newspaper articles mentioned his mood swings, his dependency on pills, and his inability to find himself in all the hype surrounding his image. They said he spent a lot of time alone in his bedroom, depressed.

I suppose that during this time I, a conservative, well-dressed, mild-mannered small-town elementary school teacher, related more closely to Elvis Presley, the King of Rock and Roll, than I did to my missionary family members. My daughters would have been beside themselves if they'd heard me say it, and I should have mentioned my affinity for Elvis if for that reason alone, just to hear them laugh.

From Panama we flew to Miami for a few luxurious days in

a beach hotel before going home. While we were in Miami, Miriam picked up a brochure on Walt Disney World, located just a few hours away in Orlando, and decided she must go. Elvira and Marj wanted to stay at the hotel and sip non-alcoholic Margaritas by the pool, and so I offered to accompany Miriam. The next morning she and I woke up at five to catch a bus headed for Orlando, for a day of "thrilling adventure we would never, ever forget," according to the pamphlet, which I added to the stack of travel brochures I had collected throughout the course of our journey, for research purposes.

This was to be our last real outing together as a father and daughter, though of course I didn't know it at the time. She was thirteen, still a child, but not for much longer. It didn't take her long to thrill to the prospect of freedom, rebellion, and independence, and I found it increasingly difficult to know where I stood in her life or what my role was supposed to be. My only advice to her ever, aside from Hang in there, baby, had been, Be yourself, and now that she was attempting to do just that, I was confused.

It had been easier to understand Marjorie as she grew from a girl to a young woman, because she was such a good kid in the traditional sense. She was involved in church youth groups and was a formidable member of the high school Reach for the Top team, especially in the areas of art, music, and history. She was chosen, from her entire school population, to attend a government-sponsored forum in Ottawa for teens from across Canada; she had won scholarships for her piano playing, had taken on a part-time job at the library, and was determined to attend university upon graduation from grade twelve. She and I regularly engaged in political debates around the kitchen table, she from her platform of socialist idealism and I from my platform of conservative pragmatism. Even her choice of history as a major at university mirrored my own interests. I was very proud of her and of her abilities.

Miriam, on the other hand, baffled me. At the age of fifteen she quit going to church and began to smoke Black Cat cigarettes. She ran around town with French boys from neighbouring communities and often snuck out of the house through her bedroom window late at night. She drank beer at the gravel pits, mouthed off at teachers she didn't like, skipped out of classes, got by with Cs, and announced she would never attend university after witnessing first-hand the stress it created for both her parents and her sister.

She and I had a great time together that day at Disney World. When I mentioned I was concerned about going on the Space Mountain roller-coaster ride, after seeing all the health warnings and signs urging the removal of hats and scarves and glasses and wigs and dentures and pacemakers and steel plates, she smiled her back-seat-of-the-Land-Rover smile and told me it would be okay, I could hold her hand. At the end of the ride I made her laugh by pretending to have been fast asleep and then asking if there wasn't something faster we could sample. I had never been more terrified, more adrenaline-filled, more awake and thankful to be alive in my life. We went on every ride she picked, and many more than once, including the giant Ferris wheel. We dangled happily in a little car twenty stories high and watched the sun set over Florida.

25

That trip marked the beginning of new chapters in the lives of Elvira and the girls as they went on to university, career, and adolescence. They had adopted modern attitudes as well, towards things like church, authority, politics, and sex. They were still my family, I loved them very much, and they loved me, but they were becoming more and more strange to me, only because they were moving easily through time and I wasn't and I didn't know what to do about it. I tried to substitute the security that a parent's unconditional love gives you with a dignified career, a beautiful home, a normal family of my own, and a Christian faith in God. I wonder if it's possible.

I completed my master's degree in education at the University of Manitoba, commuting back and forth after work for classes and seminars. The week I received my degree, Mother chose to highlight, in her newspaper column, Reg's long-ago graduation from high school, and the fact that he had been the school valedictorian. There was no mention of my degree. But then again, that was not a surprise. Mother had, over the years, often singled out the accomplishments of Reg and Diana, to the point where people would ask me from time to time if I had noticed, if it bothered me, if I had ever, perhaps, wondered why this was. I had wondered.

When it came time for Miriam to graduate from high school, I suffered another breakdown and was hospitalized here, at Bethesda. Had I been trying to avoid the inevitable reality of my youngest child leaving home, for that is what she did directly after the graduation ceremony? In fact, the only reason she had even stuck around for the convocation was for my sake, knowing that it would mean a lot to me to see her in her gown and mortarboard accepting her diploma. A day or two later, I was released from the hospital and went home to find her packing her bags, on her way to Quebec, then Europe . . . then, in her words, who knows? I was devastated, nervous, and bewildered. What would happen to her? Didn't she know that the world was a dangerous place?

That afternoon, hours before she was scheduled to catch a train to Montreal, I asked her to mow the lawn. Again, it was probably a subconscious plan to keep my youngest child from leaving the nest and altering my world. She told me she didn't really have time to mow the lawn, that she was running a bit behind. If I'd asked earlier, maybe, but now it was too late. I was adamant. I insisted that she mow the lawn one last time before she left home. I felt like a fool and a tyrant and I knew I was beginning to sound desperate and ridiculous, but I couldn't let go of this last-ditch effort to wield some type of parental authority, however pathetic it was. I refused to back down, reinforcing her desire to leave with every word that came out of my mouth: I don't think it's asking too much for you to mow the lawn one last time. Isn't it the least you could do? Am I being unreasonable? That sort of thing, until I was literally following her around the house as she threw her belongings into her bag, pleading with her mother to make me stop "with the lawn mowing thing." But I wouldn't. Never before in my life had I behaved this way with either of my girls, but that day I was out of my head. Even Elvira, who could usually calm us all down with a joke or a hastily whispered promise (Never mind, Mel, let's have a bowl of ice cream), was left shaking her head at my utter refusal to give in. Maybe you should just do it, she said to Miriam, and I'll get you to the city on time, don't worry. And then, to me, She'll do it, Mel, okay? Relax.

A few minutes later Miriam was flying around the lawn with the mower, nicking a few of my petunias and shrubbery as she careened about, looking for all the world like a psychotic killer on the loose. When she had finished I quietly retreated to my bedroom and listened to her sobbing in the kitchen, asking Elvira why I had to be that way, why I was the way I was, and Elvira saying nothing but I don't know, honey, I don't know.

She left for good that day, without either one of us saying good-bye, and I remained in my room for a long time afterwards, unsure of everything, afraid, heartbroken, overwhelmed, and hating myself.

⌒♋⌒

Hercules has left the building. Nurses have told me he will be fine. I've heard those words before, and I do not believe them. Number of things that are fine: zero. Am reminded of a newspaper article I read in *Free Press*. A psychiatric patient from St. Joseph, Missouri, claims that all his knowledge is stored in two boxcars — he quoted numbers — on the Great Western line, just outside Kansas City. Patient would like to retrieve knowledge, request denied by state hospital. Man quoted as saying: "It is too bad when a man got to use a boxcar to get out of a hospital."

I am allowed out on walks, but where will I go? Daughters mollified somewhat by the idea of me walking. They want me to have my freedom but are afraid I will get lost or hit by a car. They tell me to look both ways before crossing the street. Have told me things are looking up. That hired woman is getting things done, answers, transfers. That I will be reunited with Elvira very, very soon now. That the move is under way.

❧

Several weeks after the lawn-mowing fiasco Elvira and I sat together in lawn chairs in front of our house, staring at the traffic and waving hello to the people that passed. Elvira tried to convince me that everything would be all right, that the girls would be safe, that leaving home was a natural thing to do and that we were free now to do whatever we pleased. I had no idea what she meant by that last comment. I nodded and smiled.

❧

I continued to teach, and Elvira began a new career as a social worker with the Children's Aid Society and continued taking university courses. Our paths crossed less often. I left for school early, before she was up, and she returned late, after I had gone to bed. On the weekends, however (after I had returned from church, where I was still racking up the attendance awards), she and I would go for long drives, or watch a ball game together, or visit with friends, and our love for each other persevered.

Our girls were away, "having experiences," according to Elvira, who had trained them to believe that accumulating experiences, good or bad, was the meaning of life. I had hoped that one or both of them would want the experience of marrying a local boy, settling down within walking distance, attending church, and working part time at the bank or Penner Foods. No such luck. My girls did not come back except for short visits, during which I often remained in my bedroom while they laughed and carried on with Elvira in the kitchen, like old times. They were three women now, and they had changed. If I did emerge from my bedroom, it was only to say hello and good-bye, or to leave for a long walk. And yet I hated to see them go. It didn't make sense.

During this time we were having problems with skunks in our backyard, and it bothered me a great deal. So much so that one evening while saying grace at the supper meal, I asked God to help us find a way of getting rid of the skunks through non-violent means. Elvira actually laughed out loud mid-prayer, and, when I had finished, said: Mel, if you can pray for the well-being of skunks, can't you also pray once or twice for the well-being of your own daughters?

After that I did include my daughters in my prayers, but I felt ashamed for not having thought of it myself and embarrassed at the obvious ridiculousness of praying for skunks.

26

I have walked! We have walked! My daughter and I. We took
a circuitous route to the house — I can't bear to walk down
Main Street for fear of whom I'll meet — and indeed the
flowers are fine, the lawn has been mowed. That's a huge
relief. Inside the house, however, was another story. Empty.
Cleared out, save for a few boxes yet to be moved. My
daughter had warned me. What about all my files? I asked.
They're fine, at the new apartment. We sat together on the
kitchen floor (somebody has cleaned up the blood) and ate
Husky Burgers from Edgar's Diner. She talked about the move
as a positive thing, rubbing my shoulder intermittently in an
encouraging manner. She is getting tired. You need a nap, I
said, but there are no beds in the house. She says she isn't
tired at all, but I persuade her to curl up on the living-room
carpet and rest before we head back to the hospital. What will
you do? she asks me. I tell her, I'll be in the yard. It takes us a
long time to walk back to the hospital. I bought her an ice

cream at the A&W, as I had hundreds of times years ago, and a milkshake for myself. When we got to the hospital parking lot, I turned and began to walk away. She didn't notice for a few seconds and when she realized that I wasn't beside her, she looked over her shoulder and then stopped. Dad, she said, and I stopped too, turned around and came back to her.

After she left, the nurse came to my room with pills. A funny thing happened to me on the way to the hospital, I said in the manner of a stand-up comedian. How can you joke about it, Mel? she asked. How can you not? I answered, before swallowing my medicine.

⚬⟋⟋⟋⟋⟍⟍

During the summer of 1985, it just so happened that all four of us were in London, England, at the same time, together in a way, but not exactly. Marj was staying in a posh flat in Notting Hill with a couple of friends. Miriam was staying with her boyfriend and several other people, including a Dutch woman who ate heart, rare, twice a week, in a run-down house in Brent Cross, and Elvira and I were staying in a hotel in Russell Square, on holiday.

Marj had purchased tickets for all of us for Mozart's Requiem at St. Martin-in-the-Fields. She said this was a rare opportunity we couldn't pass up. Miriam showed up without her boyfriend at the last minute and offered to take the seat directly behind the pillar in the church. I may nap, she informed us. Later that evening the four of us wandered over to Hyde Park and joined thousands of Londoners who had come to see the spectacular bank holiday fireworks choreographed to Handel's Water Music. To be silly, we each bought one of those green reflective tubes and wore them around our necks. We were together again, if only briefly, and I remember looking up at the night sky and silently thanking God for that perfect day. After the fireworks, we all said good-bye and left in different directions for our various lodgings.

The next morning Miriam and her boyfriend picked Elvira and me up at our hotel in their 1969 (Summer of Love) Volkswagen minibus and the four of us headed off to Scotland for a few days of sightseeing. All I remember of that trip is Miriam smashing the van into a toll booth on the far side of the Humber Bridge. The steering wheel's on the wrong side for these damn things, she said, which made little sense to me. Her boyfriend changed the tire that had popped on impact with the little building, while Elvira and I made small talk with the man in the toll booth, who was understandably rattled by the experience. I didn't understand much of what he said, so thick was his Scottish brogue, but I smiled sympathetically.

Marj's life made a certain amount of sense to me, in that it seemed to be following a focused course, but again, Miriam's did not. Her experiences included several continents, little money, strange jobs, sporadic university attendance, and two children, each by a different man, neither of whom she had or has any intention, it would seem, of marrying. I've never once spoken to her about her "choices," as they're called these days, but I've been very, very troubled by them and by what people would think — that is, people in this town, my church, my mother. People whom she gives no consideration to whatsoever because I've shown her, over the years, the damage that living up to their expectations will do to a person. Or so I believe. Perhaps I haven't been such a parental disaster. Again, I've held myself up as an example of what not to become. Perhaps she's a better student than I gave her credit for.

Marj seemed to pull away from the church and this town more gradually and certainly with less obvious hostility. She didn't mind spending a week or two at home, and she found things to do and old friends to talk to while she was here. She was tolerant of the town's pace, and patient with its people.

She wasn't as quick as Miriam to denounce everything about this place as being backward, soul-destroying, hypocritical, or excruciatingly dull. And because she and I shared an interest in history and politics it was easier to have a conversation with her than with Miriam, who was critical of everything about this town and often said (vociferously announced) that it depressed the hell out of her.

What's new in this place, Dad? Miriam would ask me when she and her kids came to visit. Well, I'd say, smiling, not much. Didn't think so, she'd say, satisfied.

Sometimes, to get her to laugh, I'd say something like, Well, the town's thinking about adding another nine holes to the golf course, or, Well, there's talk of a new culvert going in behind the school. And she'd spend a good minute or two oohing and aahing for my benefit.

Elvira would race into the city regularly between work and university to spend time with the girls and the grandchildren, while I doggedly stuck to my usual routine of school and church and Mother. Both my brother and sister were living in the United States now, and so the task of taking care of Mother continued to be mine and Elvira's. Sadly, Henry, her second husband, passed away, and her drinking got worse again.

In her eighties she was becoming too feeble to make the trek to Economy Foods to nick her vanilla, but she got around the problem by ordering boxes of it through the grocery delivery service. Sometimes, in a (touching and comical) attempt to appear less obvious, she would also order a box or two of breakfast cereal, or a bag of flour to give the impression that she was doing a tremendous amount of baking. During our regular vanilla purges at Mother's apartment, Elvira and I would clear out as many as thirty boxes of breakfast cereal at a time. The number of vanilla bottles, empty or otherwise, was much higher. While we cleaned, mother would sit in her green La-Z-Boy, next to her tidy arrangements of African violets and framed photographs of family members, and gaze out the large window, towards the outskirts of town, towards her old homestead, grinning wildly from ear to ear, thinking of God knows what, or whom.

The idea of my informing my mother (twice!) that Miriam was pregnant and unmarried was unthinkable. I was desperately afraid of her reaction. Again, I felt, I had come up short of her expectations. Now, not only was I a disappointing son but I was a wretched father as well, and it was more than I could take. Each time Miriam jubilantly announced to our family that she was pregnant, I panicked and took to my bed for three or four weeks, leaving Elvira with the responsibility of breaking the news to Mother.

♾

And the years passed. I functioned more or less automatically, reciting Bible verses to my reflection as I shaved, hoping to be inspired, reading the biographies and autobiographies of various individuals, hoping to learn about life, being alone, happy at the cottage, writing notes to myself, filling my family file, walking, walking, walking, taking care of my yard and my flowerbeds, ingesting pills, practising my typing, seeing my psychiatrist, attending library meetings, attending church, attending to Mother, and teaching school. One by one Elvira's brothers, and a sister, died. Not one of them had made it much past the age of sixty. I missed my brothers-in-law intensely. Their good humour and lust for life, like Elvira's, had amused and sustained me. Lean not unto thine own understanding but trust in the Lord with all your heart and He shall direct your paths, I reminded myself countless times a day.

♾

Have just been visited by Reg and Diana. She tells me that I will have to make up my mind about how I want to live — spend my time in bed or face life. I want to ask if there are any other choices, but I smile, nod, wait, stare out the window, will the world, including them, to leave. Brother tells me he has hired a man to take care of my flowers. That explains it. Would like to say, Hire a psychiatrist to take care of your brother, but don't. Muster up the words to thank him. Would like to see my flowers one more time, very much so.

27

November 30, 1993. My heart stopped functioning properly and gave the idea to my brain.

My last day of teaching, brought on by a heart attack while hanging up Christmas decorations in the hallway at Elmdale School. I suppose I should have known it would happen there. As I descended from my stepladder, doubled over in pain and hung with garlands, Gary, the principal, happened by and asked me if I needed help. I just might, I said, hoping not to alarm the young man, I just might. He brought me here, of course, and the doctors prescribed two aspirins. Not a heart attack, they said, we're certain of it. That evening Elvira asked why, if it wasn't a heart attack, I was in so much pain and receiving large doses of morphine. The doctor upgraded my condition to a mild heart attack and said I'd be home in two or three days.

But several days later, I went into heart failure. I was rushed by ambulance to the intensive care unit of the Health Sciences Centre in Winnipeg, where they told my family I had little chance of surviving, and where I was immediately intubated, unable to breathe at all on my own. And we think, added the doctor, that he may have sustained some damage to the brain. How is that? asked the family. Loss of oxygen, said the doctor simply. We would have liked to have seen him put on a respirator sooner.

I remember lying naked in the ICU (I had a high fever and they were trying to keep me cool), hooked up to tubes and wires and IVs, unable to speak because of the hose in my throat and unable to move at all, and listening to the beautiful high voices of the Elmdale school choir singing Christmas carols. The radio station in Steinbach had taped them singing especially for me. They said, this is for Mel Toews, if he can hear us, from the students of Elmdale School who miss him very much, who want him to get well and come back to school, and who wish him a very Merry Christmas.

∽

There was a cantankerous man recovering in the area next to mine whom the nurses jokingly called Sunshine. He was a homeless man who refused to tell anybody his name and was brought in by the police after he collapsed in the street. He frequently pulled out the tubes they had attached to him and the nurses were continuously reprimanding him and telling him he might die if he didn't lie still and keep his tubes in. Do you want to die, Sunshine? they'd ask as they re-tubed him each time. Do you want to die? Go to hell, he'd say. You know you'll die if you do it again, they'd say. Good! he'd answer. I'll see you there! When the nurses had set up the radio right next to my head and turned the volume up high so I'd hear my kids singing, Sunshine hollered, Christ, turn that damn radio off! The nurses quieted him down, saying, That's okay, Sunshine, it's for Mel. I couldn't actually see Sunshine in my position on the bed but I lifted my hand slightly and waved. Go to hell, he said. But I was able to hear my students above the noise he made, singing the songs we'd rehearsed so many times for the big Christmas concert, and they sounded perfect to me, like a professional choir of angels. Even Sunshine acknowledged that they weren't half bad, but said they made him feel he'd already died and gone to heaven.

Eventually Sunshine left. For where, I have no idea. Reg had brought Mother all the way in from Steinbach to visit me in the hospital, and I did something I had never dreamt I'd have the courage to do. I refused to see her. I told Elvira I couldn't bear it. I couldn't bear to see the look on her face when she saw me hooked up to all the machines and wires and to know how disappointed she would be. Now Mel's heart fails on top of everything else! Is there no end? That sort of thing. I just couldn't do it. Elvira informed Mother that I wasn't up to having visitors, and Mother, grin fastened to her face, sat in the waiting room until Reg showed up to take her back home. My one and only act of defiance shocked Elvira and she said she was proud of me, even though the only thing I was of me was sick. Elvira and the girls took me home on Christmas Eve. They wrapped a green woollen scarf around my neck and ears and helped me out to the car, one daughter on each side of me and Elvira waiting behind the wheel with the engine running. I hadn't made a full recovery but nobody told me that then. Why ruin Christmas?

I'd like to forget the last three and a half years of my life, and, at this rate, I probably will. After a long and often fruitless search for help, Elvira finally found a specialist who gave me devastating news. He told me that I had suffered and would continue to suffer from small strokes and that I would very likely come to a point where I had no regrets and no hopes. No memory of the past and no plans for the future. What does one say? Elvira and I went for a long drive through the countryside after that particular appointment. She tried not to cry, tried to look at the bright side of things, held on to my wrists like the old days. We can travel now, Mel, we'll have fun. But I didn't say a word. Needless to say, my teaching days were over. In the beginning, for the first few months, I tried to imagine a life without teaching. My memory was bad and I easily became fearful and confused, but I tried to exercise regularly and to carry on with the work I'd been doing outside of the classroom, which included my never-ending research on important Canadians and my book on the prime ministers. I asked myself continuously how this could have happened. I was doing what I do, I thought, I was teaching school, hanging up Christmas decorations, how could this have happened?

Elvira and the girls and the grandchildren did their best to cheer me up, to keep me busy, to keep me out of bed, but gradually, and inexorably, I succumbed to the deepest, darkest depression I'd ever experienced in my life. I was nothing if not a teacher, and there was no other explanation.

Mother's drinking finally stopped the day she died, age eighty-nine, in this hospital shortly after my "retirement." When Elvira tiptoed into my bedroom to give me the news, I pretended to be asleep. Mother's gone, Mel, she whispered. And I remember thinking: Then I have nothing else left to prove, have I?

If a depressed man can grieve, then I suppose I did. I grieved for what might have been. I felt guilty for not having had the courage or the love necessary to forgive her. Somehow, I thought, that might have made a difference, but of course everything was too late now. That my wife and my daughters and their partners and various children were still very much alive, and that they loved me, and that they were becoming more desperate and worried about me with every day that passed, was a fleeting, abstract notion, compared to my all-consuming obsession with what I had lost in my life and what

I had failed to accomplish by waiting too long. There was never any doubt in my mind that it had been my sole responsibility to build a relationship with my mother, and that I had failed to do it.

In the beginning of this three-and-a-half-year period, Elvira managed to persuade me to travel with her to Arizona, to one of these gated communities in the desert where white, middle-class, retired folks go to get away from the cold winter. Naturally, this was not Elvira's idea of an adventure, but she knew it was a compromise she might pull off. It was a very safe, very conventional, very familiar place, but away from home at least. Her sister and brother-in-law went there often and so did a few other couples we knew. I agreed to it. As always, when away from home, I managed to function normally and even enjoy the odd moment here and there. While Elvira swam, played Scrabble, went on desert hikes, and took off to watch spring-training baseball games, I researched the lives of Canadians (Emily Stowe, Emily Carr, Henry Pellatt, the King of Casa Loma, and Cora Hind, to name a few) in the small library that had been set up in the common area of the "compound." (My daughter's word for it. I'd call it a trailer park.)

I made a few phone calls, one to Llew, my mechanic, to tell him how well the car was running, and to Elmdale School to make arrangements with Miss Hill that she would put chocolate bars on the staffroom table when she thought the time would be right, and that I'd reimburse her when I got back. I updated my diary. I visited with other compound-dwellers, I sat by the pool in the sun and attended the occasional lecture on holistic health or whatever was being offered. From time to time the activity director would arrange for a nurse to ride around on what looked like a Dickie-Dee ice cream bike from trailer to trailer offering the oldies various medical tests and advice. Oh my, hooted Elvira the first time she saw the nurse on the bike, it's come to this! I read up on the Reichmanns, the Bronfmans, the Cronkites, and the Gores, and Arizona: a cavalcade of history. And I walked.

Elvira decided it would be great to have the grandchildren come and visit us during their spring break, and she immediately went about making the arrangements. We all had a wonderful time. Elvira and the kids flew about from one activity to the next and I, in my usual way, watched them from the sidelines, amused and bewildered. I particularly enjoyed sitting by the pool and watching the kids swim. The oldies rarely swam. They stood, like storks, in waist-high water, wearing straw hats and working at crossword puzzles, while my grandchildren darted around them, underwater, like electric eels. Eventually, one of the oldies would glance meaningfully at me from under his or her boater, and I'd casually suggest to the kids that we head back to the trailer for some lunch.

The kids were hugely amused by the type of activities and games we residents participated in. My grandson suggested we throw all our medication into one big pile and, when signalled, run towards it, scramble to find our own, and run back to the starting line — the objective, of course, to do it in the least amount of time. I assured him that I'd bring it up with the activity director that very afternoon.

When we returned home, on April 4, 1997, the writing and the walking stopped. Got home to 58 Brandt Rd. in Steinbach at 5:50 p.m., reads the last entry of my travel journal. I think we should have kept on going perhaps, from one compound to another if nothing else, just staying away from Steinbach and everything it meant. But that's a type of lifestyle that didn't make any sense to me then, a vagabond's life on the road, moving from place to place.

⁓

Speaking of moving from place to place, I've just come back from the morgue. (And how many of us can say that?) I didn't mean to go there, but somehow I got lost, trying to find a place to walk without activating alarms. My daughter will come later and walk with me outside, but in the meantime I felt as though I'd explode if I didn't walk. I got on an elevator, pushed several buttons, like a kid, and moments later the elevator door opened in the basement, next to the underground tunnel that links the main hospital with the personal care home for seniors. I walked for a while through this empty concrete sterile tube until I heard the voices of children. I stopped dead in my tracks and wondered where I was. For a second I worried that I hadn't prepared my lessons for the day. There was a slight bend in the tunnel, and the voices were coming from beyond this bend. I could also hear a sound that I thought was a toy car being driven back and forth along the concrete, something, anyway, with wheels. I didn't know what to do or where to go. Then, from a distance of about a hundred yards, I saw a child fly up into the air in a crouching position and drop down again, unharmed. Then more children appeared, and they all seemed to be moving in circles around the inside of the tunnel, upside down and around and around, entirely unaffected by the laws of gravity. It was a lovely sight.

I stood very still and watched them. At first, I was afraid they would hurt themselves, but then, after a few minutes, I began to relax and enjoy myself. I didn't know what was happening but the children seemed to know what they were doing and they appeared to be having a wonderful time. Suddenly, one of the children, a boy of about thirteen, looked over to where I was standing, and I could hear him call out to his friends, but I wasn't sure of what he was saying. I panicked, thinking that by startling them I had risked their safety, and quickly looked around for a place to hide. There was a door next to me, one I hadn't noticed earlier, and I pushed through it, realizing instantly that I was in the morgue. Then I went through a rather sci-fi-ish episode of wondering whether I was dead and if the tunnel I had just been in was the tunnel they mention in stories of near-death experiences and whether or not the children were angels or versions of me or just what in the Sam Hill was going on. I stood in the room, surrounded by stainless steel drawers and cabinets and instruments, feeling relieved that it was over, that it wasn't so bad after all, until I heard my name being called. Mr. Toews, came a boy's voice from the hallway, is that you? No, I thought of saying, it isn't! (I don't know what's become of him!) but instead I remained quiet, hoping that the boy wouldn't enter the morgue and suffer the shock of finding me dead, but looking alive, or rather, finding me alive but feeling dead. Regardless, I didn't want him to see me. I leaned, softly, against one of the drawers and closed my eyes, and waited. And while I waited, I prayed that God would forgive me for all that I had failed to accomplish, and that he would understand that I simply could not go on. I prayed for deliverance, and forgiveness yet again, and for some sign of understanding. I prayed that in spite of everything, I would be understood. That's the last thing I remember of the morgue, but miraculously I am still alive and back in my room.

I have no idea what happened, how I got back here, or why. Am rather disappointed, after all, but grateful of course to have been helped. I will attempt to ask daughters, without alarming them, what the dickens happened to me down there.

28

At home I stayed in bed. When the girls and the grandchildren came to visit, Elvira would plead with me to get out of bed, to make an appearance at least and say hello. I'd gamely throw on a bathrobe and stumble down the hallway towards the living room like a modern-day Lear, wild hair and eyes, unshaven, and barely coherent. Eventually even that became too much for me and the girls and the grandkids came to my bedroom to say hello, though often I was unable, or unwilling, to respond at all. They'd sit on the edge of my bed, chatting about their lives, offering to bring me a glass of water or a roll with butter, which, in addition to Snickers bars, was all that I ate. Elvira would stash several of the bars in the cupboard next to my pills where she knew I would find them. I had long ago stopped sitting at the table with her at regular mealtimes. If I wanted to get up and eat something I would do it at night, while she slept. She continued to prepare the meals I had enjoyed before, however, hoping that I'd change my mind, which I rarely did.

Sometimes, in the evening, she was able to persuade me to sit on the loveseat with her for half an hour or so, and we'd hold hands and look out the large living-room window and talk about happier times and the possibilities for fun that lay ahead. Well, she talked about them and I nodded occasionally or smiled. She told me there would be more happy times, that we would weather this storm together just the way we had weathered all the others. Remember, she said, when I used to hide your alarm clocks so you'd stay in bed with me just a little bit longer?

I played with her gold bracelet, a gift I'd given her a year or so earlier, while she talked. It was all I could do to show her I was listening, that I loved her. Later in the evening, Elvira would join me in bed and take my hand and put it on her wrist and I'd move the fragile chain around and around and Elvira would say I love you too, Mel. Try to have a good sleep. At night, often, I would wake her because something had frightened me, a sound, a bad dream, or a premonition that something had happened to her, or the girls, or the grand-children. She would reassure me that all was well and go back to sleep until I woke her again, fearful of yet another imagined threat or impending disaster.

During the day she continued to work as a therapist, seeing clients in her small office, Marj's former bedroom, while I lay in my bed and waited for her to be finished. More irony: Elvira had earned a master's degree in marriage and family therapy and was now helping other people get their lives together, even as ours were falling apart. I was unaware of her own increasing level of exhaustion. I needed her too badly for that. There are no windows within the dark house of depression through which to see others, only mirrors.

My youngest grandchild loved to bring me my pills in a small painted eggcup, and I forced myself to smile and thank her each time. I wanted her to stay with me and sing her crazy, impassioned songs or to tell me one or many of her stories. Grandpa, she'd say, I'll give you a choice: scary, sad, funny, or scary. I knew she loved to tell the scary ones. How about scary, I'd say. But not too scary, I'll have bad dreams. Okay, she'd say and launch into the most bizarre and violent tale you could imagine coming from a six-year-old. Sometimes she would wander around and around my bedroom as she told her stories, in a type of creative trance. Sometimes she would jump up and down lightly on the bed as she told them, and as my heavy body moved up and down to the gentle rhythm of her bouncing, I would close my eyes and pretend I was on a boat at sea. I wanted her to leave immediately, to switch off the light and close the door behind her, to stop torturing me with the lightness and beauty of her being.

I had stopped going out for walks. I was too ashamed of myself, of what I'd become, and the very idea of discussing my so-called health or retirement with other robust and working men and women of my age, terrified me. I stopped going to church. Understandably, many friends and relatives had given up on me as an interesting person to visit, although their prayers, they assured me, would continue. But my minister kept coming by. He came to the house often, even after I'd begged Elvira not to allow any visitors inside. He sat on the sofa and told me many things, that God loved me, that he loved me, that my faith would see me through this time, and though I didn't say a word save for the rare whispered thank you, I appreciated those visits more than he will ever know.

In the meantime, I kept my doctors' appointments, and continued to tell the doctors that I was okay. I might mention that my energy was low, or that it wasn't what it should be, or that retirement can be a difficult time in a man's life, or other vague complaints along those lines, but nothing more. I managed to pull myself together for these appointments and if I simply couldn't, I asked Elvira to cancel them. Otherwise, I would arrive at the clinic washed, shaved, friendly, and well dressed. And then I'd act the part. If Elvira attempted (going to great efforts not to embarrass me) to convey the truth, for instance by telling the doctor, Well, he's not entirely okay, really, I can't get him to eat, or, This is actually the first time he's been out of bed in several weeks, then the doctor would look to me for confirmation and I would only smile. I don't think it was clear to him exactly what was going on. He didn't know whom to believe, and I, after all, was the patient. If I said I was okay, only a bit tired now and again, well then . . . It was an awkward situation for all of us: Elvira was growing desperate and exhausted, wanting some type of help taking care of me, keeping me alive, but at the same time not wanting to admit defeat and afraid that I would misinterpret her request for outside care as a lack of love.

She was also trying to protect my privacy and my extreme pride. She knew I loathed the idea of anybody, other than her, taking care of my needs and feared that my depression would get even worse if that were to happen. She had taken care of me for forty years and wasn't about to quit. In this town, a good Mennonite wife is always more than capable of taking care of her husband. It's held to be her duty and her life, and Elvira, in spite of her independence and liberal views, couldn't move from under that yoke. And I said nothing to the doctor, nothing that might have lightened her load and given her an out, because I didn't want her not to be there with me every step of the way. It's clear to me now and I wonder: Who takes care of the good Mennonite wife?

 ✑

Aha! My daughter has informed me that indeed I got "a little lost" in the hospital tunnel. She doesn't say in a psychotic state, my daughter, she says I was "a little confused." And the children? I ask. Dad, she says, do you know what they were doing? No, I answer, they were flying around the tunnel, happily, that's all I really know. My daughter, smiling, says, Those kids were skateboarding! A couple of them were students of yours and they recognized you!

Horrors. I smiled and said, Oh really. . .

Continue plan to creep up on brain. Organic shock treatment, all natural. Recall the words of Ulysses S. Grant, in his attack at Vicksburg: With speed and audacity, men, we will win.

29

The situation at home became critical. Elvira's own health had begun to suffer. Once, in Arizona, she was hospitalized briefly with dangerously high blood pressure. (Her sister, who was staying in a trailer nearby, had insisted that she go to the doctor after Elvira had passed out at the end of an uphill hike in 105-degree heat.) The doctor diagnosed her chest pain and shortness of breath as angina. He prescribed nitroglycerin puffers and patches and pills. Her gait, once brisk, slowed to a shuffle, and she stopped talking about better days ahead. She cried often to the girls, to her friends, to herself, but never to me.

She was becoming depressed too, she said, she was utterly exhausted and was on the verge of giving up and joining me in bed. The girls again insisted that she go on a holiday, and she wearily agreed, not caring where she went. When she was gone, Marj would stay with me and essentially play the same role that Elvira had, trying to get me to eat, to exercise a little, to talk. But even with the occasional visit to friends in the States or to Minneapolis for a ball game, during which she felt guilty for not being at home, Elvira was coming apart. By this time, I refused to leave my bed, other than to use the washroom, and for how much longer even that would last, I didn't know. I was eating, at most, half a bun a day, although bizarrely I continued, without fail, to take my medication, which had been increased to twenty-two pills a day. They had been prescribed to me, after all. The diagnosis: dementia, due to small strokes, exacerbated by underlying organic condition of manic depression, or vice versa, paranoia, I can't remember. Call it madness. Elvira asked me: Mel, do you want to die? No, I'd whisper. Then won't you eat a little? she'd ask. Silence. I was afraid of life and death, stuck in an excruciating limbo that seemed eternal. I had stopped keeping my doctor's appointments, and I had stopped going to church. So much for my perfect attendance record. The girls became alarmed and made several appointments of their own with my doctor, trying to explain to him the urgency of the situation, that something had to change, that this could not go on, that Elvira was going down and needed rescuing, that I would starve to death, and soon.

Eventually I agreed with them. I managed to tell Elvira that I felt as though the lights were going out, that my life was coming to an end, and that I probably should be hospitalized.

Well, we're not sure, the doctor would say, I mean he's depressed, but other than that, I mean other than making sure he's fed, I don't know exactly what . . . I could increase his medication, I suppose, although . . . I'm just not sure what we can do.

❦

That would be something though, said my daughters, feeding him, don't you understand? It would be a good start. Please, please admit him. My doctor, whether he believed them or not, agreed to have me admitted to the hospital, where in order to appear well enough to go home again, and because I was afraid of what the people I encountered in the hospital, so many of whom I'd known for years, would think, I ate, washed, shaved, and "acted normal." Again, many of the doctors and nurses felt sure that my wife and daughters had been overreacting, that perhaps they were just tired of the inconvenience of having to be with me, that perhaps they themselves had brought on my depression.

Elvira, after bringing me here and sitting beside me on this narrow bed, holding my hand, and telling me everything would eventually be fine, went to my daughter's house in the city to rest. Please don't go, I begged, following her into the hallway. Mel, she said, grabbing my wrists and bringing my arms around her in an embrace, I'll be back.

The next day, after persuading the nurses to let me go, I went back to the house, and she wasn't there. My files were in boxes and there was blood on the kitchen floor and I had lost my mind.

But you talk to her on the phone every morning, say my daughters. You know she's alive. How do I explain to them that I don't know anything anymore, and that in my mind I hear Elvira's voice often, not only on the phone in the morning but all day and all night long.

Daughters tell me I'll be transferred to the city, to a place where I'll get help, in a week to ten days. That's not long, Dad, they say, you can do it. How to tell them it may as well be ten years. And tomorrow you'll see Mom, they've agreed to let us bring you into the city for the day and she can't wait to see you. By June for sure you'll be living with her again and she's found an apartment that you'll both love, there's an activity room, and a swimming pool, and it's close to a library, and the new ballpark, won't it be good?

My plan to gradually sneak up on my brain by remembering

the past and then by seamlessly tying it into the present has not been successful. I had meant to catch it off guard by sneaking up from behind, by surprising it into submission. No such luck.

I have given Miriam some notes to give to the children, Keep up the good work in school, I hear you're a baseball hero, Would love some more art to add to "Summer Memories," Love . . .

For days I have told the girls that I love them and they have assured me they will pass my best regards on to the menfolk. Have told Elvira, I love you. I love you. I love you. What more can I say to prepare them?

✑

This extended stay at Bethesda has given me a lot of time to think, and even though I'm not the best at that these days, I feel I've reached a conclusion or two because of it.

What I would like to say to Reg but can't is that he's not to blame for being born or for being loved, and my anger and my jealousy mean nothing, but I want what he had. I'm sixty-two years old and still wanting my mother to hold me in her arms just once and tell me that she loves me. I'm a ridiculous old man. It's not her fault, either, how could it be, with ghosts and demons circling round her brain and no weapons to fight them off, nothing but a Bible, a bottle, and a perpetual grin. It's just something that happens sometimes, a story as old as time, and this time it happened to me.

✑

If Elvira is not dead, if I have not killed her, if she is still thinking about freedom or insanity, mulling it over in the city where she's resting, I would say to her: Freedom, sweetheart.

Develop a new life strategy.

Like this, through the wall, Mr. Toews, tuck your head in so you don't break your neck, through the walls and out, it will feel so good to get some fresh air.

Patient granted Leave of Absence. Has promised to return to hospital for medication, would like to see his "pink house" (?) again. Refuses to elaborate.

Number of days in hospital: seventeen. Will dress for walk. 8:27 a.m. Beautiful sun. Re May, date? Find newspaper and insert.

(And best of luck to Hercules. Avoid peanuts and ice cubes.)

As Ever, M.

Epilogue

On May 13, my father got out of bed, dressed, ate breakfast, and left the hospital. He may have taken one last walk through town, past his school and church and home perhaps, but maybe not. If he had met anyone he knew I'm almost certain he would have greeted them in his loud, friendly voice and wished them well. At some point after heading down the highway that leads out of town, he became tired of walking and hitched a ride to a pretty little town called Woodridge, about thirty miles southeast of Steinbach in the heart of Sandilands Forest. There's a café in Woodridge and a small church with a steeple that rises up above the pine trees, a cemetery, and rail tracks that run behind the café.

The waitress at the café said my father spoke to her through the back screen door. "How long before the next train?" he asked, polite as ever. "Just a few minutes," she answered. "Yes," he said, "I can hear the whistle."

Some say he knelt on the tracks, facing the little church, with his back to the oncoming train, and others say he waited until the last minute before throwing himself on the rails. An item in the next day's *Winnipeg Free Press* described him as "an unidentified, tall, older man."

Several weeks after his death, my mother went to the café to talk to the young waitress. The two of them went out back to the tracks for a look at what would have been my father's last "picture" of the world. The waitress hugged my mom and said, "Isn't it a beautiful place to leave this Earth and meet God?" These words were an amazing gift from a perfect stranger, who would have had every right to be angry and upset, and I'll always be grateful.

The only certain thing we know about that day is that the sun was shining beautifully, and that it was exceptionally warm for May 13. And that, even after his body was removed, there remained scattered on the tracks and in the ditches on each side of it several bright yellow recipe cards for writing notes. For as long as I can remember, he wrote notes to himself on cards like these before going to bed, carefully arranging them on top of his shoes where he'd be sure to find them the next morning. Sadly, the yellow cards that fell out of his pocket and onto the tracks were blank.

∽

In the end, words couldn't save my father, but his lifelong faith in the power of reading and writing will live on. In the summer of 2000, the brand-new Melvin C. Toews Reading Garden will open in Steinbach, adjacent to the public library that he was so instrumental in founding, courtesy of the Friends of the Library committee and others who have contributed time, ideas, and money. And the Elmdale School grade six students are planting dozens of red and white petunias at the Reading Garden on May 31, my father's birthday. I have no doubt that it will be beautiful, and that "Mr. Toews," if he could see it, would be tickled pink.

Dad, you've earned your rest. Schlope schein.